Performance Appraisal

Financial Times Management Briefings are happy to receive proposals from individuals who have expertise in the field of management education.

If you would like to discuss your ideas further, please contact Andrew Mould, Commissioning Editor.

Tel: 0171 447 2210
Fax: 0171 240 5771
e-mail: andrew.mould@pitmanpub.co.uk

FINANCIAL TIMES

Management Briefings

Performance Appraisal

BERNARD WYNNE

Human Resources

FT

PITMAN
PUBLISHING

London • Hong Kong • Johannesburg • Melbourne • Singapore • Washington DC

PITMAN PUBLISHING
128 Long Acre, London WC2E 9AN
Tel: +44 (0)171 447 2000
Fax: +44 (0)171 240 5771

A Division of Pearson Professional Limited

First published in Great Britain 1997

ISBN 0 273 63190 X

British Library Cataloguing in Publication Data
A CIP catalogue record for this book can be obtained from the British Library.

10 9 8 7 6 5 4 3 2 1

Printed and bound in Great Britain

The Publishers' policy is to use paper manufactured from sustainable forests.

CONTENTS

ABOUT THE AUTHOR

Bernard Wynne is Principal of Bernard Wynne Associates and Director of The European Mentoring Centre.

Following a background in human resources and management development in financial services, Bernard moved into consultancy in 1988; he was a director of The ITEM Group plc before establishing Bernard Wynne Associates in 1994.

He consults widely in the areas of HR, management development, performance management and performance improvement through quality and service excellence, across all business sectors. He has considerable experience of working with managers in skill development workshops on a wide range of subjects including behavioural and communications skills, coaching, mentoring and facilitating.

He writes extensively on HR and management development topics and has contributed chapters to *The Handbook of Training and Development*, on Evaluation of Training and *The Handbook of Management Development*, on Coaching and Mentoring.

The author can be contacted at:

180 Blackfen Road,
Sidcup,
Kent DA15 8PT
UK

Tel: 0181 850 6458
Fax: 0181 850 8974

Chapter 1

WHY APPRAISE?

INTRODUCTION

Someone once said that the person who sets out on a journey with no clear idea of where they are going is unlikely to get there. The same is true of an organisation and, of course, of individuals in organisations. Success in business, whether for the organisation, the business unit or the individual, depends on knowing the goal, purpose and direction, on knowing the capabilities of the people, and on being able to understand and measure past performance in order to plan to achieve continuous improvement in the future.

Organisations engage in a business planning cycle and likewise individual business managers need to help their people engage in a personal review of the recent past and in setting some plans for the future. This review of the past and planning for the future takes place in the majority of organisations with greater or less effectiveness, depending on a whole range of factors. This report will help you to:

- understand the purpose and benefits to be gained from effective performance appraisal;

- develop and introduce a system of performance appraisal if one does not exist in your organisation;

- understand key criteria in setting performance measures;

- understand some of the skills and techniques required in conducting performance appraisals;

- identify some of the potential pitfalls and barriers which get in the way of effective performance appraisal.

An important underlying premise on which the report is based is that *any system, no matter how good, is in reality only as good as the people who operate it.* Therefore, the world's best performance appraisal system is only as good as the managers who have to make it work. Far too many organisations assume that the ability to appraise effectively comes naturally to all those they appoint as managers and team leaders. Employees know differently.

If we were looking to identify some of the reasons why performance appraisal does not always live up to the expectations which organisations have for it, the major reason we would identify would be related to how the system is applied in practice. What organisations should be seeking to do when introducing or reviewing an appraisal system is to ensure, through training, that the appraisers are properly equipped to make the most effective use of the system.

WHAT IS PERFORMANCE APPRAISAL?

Performance appraisal is a systematic and structured approach to assessing the past performance of employees, and an attempt to influence the future performance of employees from a management perspective. Just as importantly, from the perspective of an individual employee it provides an opportunity to consider where you are and where you want to be and what actions are required to help you to bridge this gap.

When people are caught up in the day-to-day routine of a job, it can be difficult to make time to stand back and consider how they are doing. An appraisal provides this opportunity because it demands that a certain amount of time is set aside to ensure it happens. The frequency of appraisal differs from organisation to organisation and is something which is considered later; for now, it is sufficient to say that time should be set aside to review past performance and plan for the future.

THE PURPOSE OF PERFORMANCE APPRAISAL

The purpose of performance appraisal may differ from one organisation to another; for example, some organisations use the appraisal as a basis for performance related pay, while others believe that appraisal should be related to an employee's motivation and not have any overt relationship to pay. Some organisations go so far as to conduct two appraisals: one related to assessing and measuring performance and setting objectives for the future and the other to considering the personal and career development of the individual.

The actual purpose of any specific appraisal system must be related to the requirements and objectives of the organisation. It is, however, possible to identify some key considerations which will usually be included as reasons for appraisal. In most cases these will include:

- To review past and present performance, identifying strengths and weaknesses.
- To provide feedback to the individual regarding how their performance is perceived.
- To assess future promotability and potential.
- To assess training needs.
- To plan for career development.
- To assess and develop individual abilities.
- To provide an objective basis on which to base decisions about training, promotion and pay.
- To provide an opportunity for career counselling.
- To motivate employees.
- To clarify, for the individual, organisational expectations.
- To provide an opportunity for the individual to raise questions and concerns.

- To set objectives for the next period.
- To help achieve corporate and personal objectives in a planned and controlled way.
- To assist with succession planning.

As can be seen from above, the precise and particular reasons for any individual appraisal system may vary. What is important, however, is that each organisation thinks through what it is seeking to achieve and ensures that the appraisal system it introduces enables it to achieve these objectives.

WHO SHOULD BE APPRAISED?

In thinking through the purpose of the performance appraisal one of the considerations which will need to be borne in mind is who should be appraised?

Traditionally, many organisations appraised only management; others moved on from this to include all of those in *white collar* or *staff* jobs. More recently, however, organisations have realised the value of appraising all employees and many organisations now appraise all of their employees from the top to the bottom of the workforce. If a key purpose of the appraisal is to seek to explore ways to improve performance then it is easy to see why it is necessary to appraise everyone. In any case, as the rather false boundaries of the past fall away we have come to recognise that all employees have an important contribution to make to the success of the organisation and anything which helps to focus on and improve this contribution will be important.

In today's world a progressive management would be seeking to assess and raise the performance of all the people and should be more concerned to ask why are we not appraising a particular group rather than ask why they should be appraised.

A relatively small number of organisations only use appraisal to monitor the progress of poor performers. Such systems are usually based on the idea that it is only necessary for the poor performers to participate in an appraisal interview. This view is obviously so short sighted that it has, in the main, fallen into disuse. The opportunity for all employees to discuss their performance, strengths and weaknesses and plans for the future is so obviously beneficial to the individual and the organisation that just to concentrate on the poor performers is clearly an error.

WHO OWNS THE APPRAISAL?

This question raises one of the biggest problems with performance appraisal. Traditionally the personnel or human resource department has been responsible for initiating, administering and monitoring the appraisal system. In practice this has meant that personnel has been responsible for sending out the appraisal forms and reminders, providing training and collecting the completed forms.

Because the personnel department initiates the process, it appears in the eyes of many people to own it. A major reason why many systems are less effective than they should be is because they are perceived to be owned by the personnel department. Come time for the appraisal and many a manager can be heard to say, *'Personnel have sent this form down for me to complete and we have to have a chat about it first. It's not important, they just need to keep their records straight.'* Such comments, which unfortunately are not all that unusual, are often the main reason why appraisal systems don't work.

As can be seen above in the section on the purpose of appraisal, by far the most important reasons for conducting an appraisal are the potential benefits it can deliver to the individual being appraised and the manager or team leader who is responsible for doing the appraisal.

The role of the personnel department is important but secondary; there is a need for administration, monitoring and the collection of data, but this must not supersede the most important element in the appraisal relationship: that of the appraiser and appraisee. Any system which does not put this element at the centre of the process is doing less than justice to the gains to be obtained from having a system in the first place.

The design of many systems places too much importance on the role of the centre at the expense of the local, and is to blame for managers and team leaders not feeling that the appraisal belongs to them and their people. The role of the personnel department in seeming at times to act as the final arbiter of appraisal scores in some systems also creates problems of ownership.

A problem which has been identified in some cases is the way in which the appraiser is often cast in the role of 'god', having to make judgements they don't feel comfortable making, and even worse, having to hand these judgements down to people they work with on a day-to-day basis. A further difficulty is that appraisers far too often do not receive any training in the specific skills of appraisal interviewing. It is assumed that conducting an appraisal comes naturally and yet training can greatly ease the difficulty appraisers face in handling what are often uncomfortable situations. Giving face-to-face feedback does not come naturally to many people and the opportunity to practise, in a non-threatening environment, can significantly improve the skills of the appraiser. The issue of training will be covered in more detail in Chapter 10 of this report.

Any system of appraisal which does not place the ownership of the appraisal firmly in the hands of the appraisee and appraiser will deliver less than satisfactory results. This means that the design of the system and the communications which surround it must emphasise the role of the appraiser and the appraisee and play down the role of the central administering department.

Performance appraisal can only really be effective if ownership is seen to clearly reside at the local level and deliver the main benefits at this same level. The essential relationship is that between the manager or team leader and the appraisee. Performance improvement delivers results at this level with the appraisee needing to be clear about the answer to the question

'How am I doing?', an answer which can only come from the immediate supervisor. In the same way performance improvements which are agreed during the appraisal interview will be achieved on the job, through support and coaching by the appraiser.

WHO BENEFITS FROM PERFORMANCE APPRAISAL?

The benefits are, of course, closely related to the question of ownership and we will consider, below, the benefits to the individual, to the manager or team leader and to the organisation as a whole.

Benefits to the individual

Attitude and communication surveys in many organisations reveal that employees want to gain a better understanding of their role, to know what is expected of them, to know how they are assessed and, perhaps most importantly of all, to know how they are doing.

All of these questions can be answered at the appraisal interview. People perform better when they know where they fit in and when they have a clear perception of what they are expected to do. For the individual, the benefits of appraisal include:

- Getting a greater insight into their job role.
- Getting a better idea of where they fit in.
- An increased awareness of how performance is assessed and monitored.
- Gaining an insight into how their performance is perceived.
- Deepening their understanding of their strengths and weaknesses.
- Identifying ways in which to improve performance.
- Providing an opportunity to raise problems and ask questions.
- Providing an opportunity to discuss and clarify training needs.
- Enabling objectives to be set for the next period.
- Providing an opportunity to discuss career direction and prospects.

Benefits to the manager/team leader

Too much central control and direction of the appraisal process has led many managers/team leaders to fail to understand the benefits they stand to gain from appraisal. To change this they have to grasp ownership and make appraisal work for them and the people they are appraising.

The benefits are substantial and include:

- An opportunity to exchange views and opinions with team members away from the normal pressures of work.

- An opportunity to identify weaknesses and potential trouble spots.
- An improved understanding of the resources available.
- An improved understanding of the expectations and aspirations of the team.
- An opportunity to plan for and set objectives for the next period.
- An opportunity to think about their own role.
- An opportunity to plan for achieving improved performance.
- An opportunity to review and plan for further delegation and coaching.
- An opportunity to motivate members of the team.

Benefits to the organisation

The organisation stands to gain much from an appraisal system which perhaps explains why, in many cases, the organisational benefit has been over-emphasised at the expense of the benefit to the individual.

Organisational benefits include:
- A structured means of identifying and assessing potential.
- Up-to-date information regarding the expectations and aspirations of employees.
- Information on which to base decisions about promotion, motivation and pay.
- An opportunity to update succession planning.
- Information about training needs which can act as a basis for developing training plans.
- Updating of employee records.
- Career counselling.

The benefits identified for all three parties are only a sample of those which can be obtained as organisations develop systems which fulfil their specific needs. The important thing to bear in mind is that central to an effective appraisal system is the way in which it is perceived by those whom it most affects: the employees and the managers/team leaders. If these groups don't perceive the appraisal as meeting their needs, the system will not work.

APPRAISAL AND PERFORMANCE MANAGEMENT

Appraisal on its own cannot manage the performance of all employees throughout the year. In fact, it works best when it is a part of a more comprehensive system of managing performance. In recent years there has been a growth in the number of organisations introducing performance management systems. The idea of performance management has grown as organisations have responded to the need to take a more integrated approach to managing performance through objectives, rewards, knowledge, skill and competence. A system of performance management helps to pull together all the elements which influence the performance of the organisation and the individual.

Performance should, of course, be managed on an ongoing basis and it is clearly a line management responsibility. It can be influenced by a whole range of factors including environment, motivation, morale, reward, competence and management style, to name just a few. It is in recognition of the fact that performance is influenced by this package of elements which drives the need to apply an integrated approach to managing it. The idea that a once or twice a year appraisal is sufficient to manage performance is clearly ludicrous, no matter how effective the appraisal system. Appraisal, however, is an essential management tool for the effective management of performance in support of the integrated approach.

The most effective appraisal systems are those which operate as part of a wider, integrated approach to managing performance.

Chapter 2

INFORMAL AND FORMAL SYSTEMS

INFORMAL APPRAISAL

An essential part of any manager's/team leader's job is to monitor and appraise the performance of the members of their team. It is equally important to provide feedback to the individual, in order that they can take action to improve performance or change behaviour in line with the changing demands of the job. This, it is argued, is what appraisal is about, and it should go on all of the time and should not require a formal process to make it happen.

No one, with any sense, could disagree with these sentiments – they are so patently obvious. The problem, however, is that while the sentiments are true, the reality in practice is frequently far from satisfactory. As in so many areas of management, the stated ideal is often far from the practice. Good management certainly demands that the manager regularly appraises the members of the team, but the question has to be asked: how many, in fact, do?

As the saying goes, *'The road to hell is paved with good intentions.'* In the same way, what a manager intends to do is often knocked off track by surrounding events. The intention to appraise and provide feedback to team members is often there, but in reality, given the various competing pressures on management time, it is frequently the one priority which gets overlooked.

In reviewing the results of employee attitude surveys in different organisations, one is often struck by two recurring themes.

1. The number of people who say: *'The trouble with this place is that, you are always told when you do something wrong, but nobody ever gives you praise and credit when you do something well.'*

2. The number of people who say: *'I have very little idea of how my performance is seen. I imagine it is alright, otherwise someone would tell me, wouldn't they?'*

We can see from these two statements that many managers are not very good at giving feedback; thus, to leave the appraisal process to the informal interchange between managers and staff may lead to it not happening at all.

This is the negative argument against informal systems. There is, however, also a positive argument against.

Formal systems cannot and should not seek to replace the ongoing informal process of review and feedback between managers and team members as a team or as individuals. What a formal system can seek to do, in the worst case, is to ensure that at least at regular intervals managers have to sit down and conduct some form of appraisal. In the best case, of course, the formal review can provide a focal point, away from the day-to-day pressures of work, to allow for a joint discussion about issues of performance, development and motivation. In this best case example, the formal appraisal does not replace the informal; it enhances it, places it on record and formalises actions coming out of it which need to be taken by, either or both, the manager and the individual.

The issue then, regarding informal systems, is that they are an essential part of the practice of good management. They are, however, only one part of the ongoing process of reviewing performance and always benefit from being complemented and supported by a formal system.

A FORMAL SYSTEM

A formal system, by definition, has to have procedures and controls, have records and administration, and should, at least, be applied uniformly across whole divisions, if not in fact across whole organisations.

A formal system of appraisal will include:

- A set of procedures which will outline the process to be followed.

- Some form of central administration to send out forms and collect data.

- A form to be completed.

- An agreed time to hold the appraisal interview.

Each of these elements will now be outlined in more detail.

APPRAISAL PROCEDURES

The procedures surrounding appraisal should be kept as simple as possible: no one likes building unnecessary bureaucracy and this is especially true where the need for the procedures is to support and encourage the effective use of a process. Having said that, however, unless everyone plays the same tune, the process will not be seen by the users as being fair and equal to all.

The procedures need to cover:

- An explanation of how the appraisal will take place, who will do it and will anyone else be involved. Where will it take place? Will there be an appraisal discussion/interview? Some appraisal systems require the manager to complete a form assessing an individual, but do not include an interview as a necessary part of the process. This report will not be concerned with systems of this type, as they are not considered to be very useful. A discussion providing an opportunity for two-way feedback is considered to be an essential part of the process.

- When it will take place. What preparation will be required by the appraiser and by the appraisee? What happens to the form and the data after the interview?

- In some cases, where the system requires an element of merit rating which may have an impact on pay, the procedures may need to outline what will happen in the case of a disputed rating.

Central administration

This is the cause of many of the problems with the ownership of appraisal systems. Someone has to design, manage and administer the process. Without this central administration a formal process will not work. In most organisations the personnel or human resource department provides this service. This leads, as noted in Chapter 1, many people to believe that because they administer the process they also own it.

The central coordination is important for data gathering and analysis, for updating employee records, for drawing together information regarding succession planning and training needs. The style which should be encouraged from the central coordination is one which implies support for the management application of the process, not control.

The appraisal form

An appraisal form is important for a number of reasons, including providing a structure for the interview and for recording the data which will be discussed. There are many types of appraisal form and a number of examples will be discussed in Chapter 6.

An agreed time for the interview

Organisations differ about when to hold appraisal interviews, with some conducting interviews for each employee on the anniversary date of when that employee joined the organisation or on the employee's birth date. By far the majority, however, conduct all the interviews within a set period of time, usually an agreed four to six weeks. As more organisations move towards having some link between performance and appraisal it will become more logical to have a set annual date for appraisal.

An example of procedure notes to cover an appraisal system is given in Appendix A.

DEFINING PERFORMANCE

There is a tendency for many managers to use a word like performance as though what it means is clear and agreed by all of those concerned. The reality is rather different and how performance is assessed is a highly contentious issue about which there is often little agreement.

A major concern of many people is that different appraisers will assess performance in different ways, with some being soft and others being hard. It will always be the case that some element of appraisal will be subjective as it is almost impossible to envisage a system which is wholly objective. For this reason, when designing a system, it is important to define, as closely as possible, just what is meant by performance. This can be done by establishing performance criteria, which should be agreed as widely as possible across the organisation.

Performance criteria

Performance criteria can be described as falling broadly into three types: criteria which seek to measure personality characteristics, criteria which seek to measure performance characteristics, and the achievement of previously agreed objectives.

The use of personality characteristics often includes the appraiser being asked to assess such things as loyalty, integrity, energy and determination, for example. One can see the difficulty this type of approach would create for appraisers who have different personal perceptions of what such words mean. People who have experience of this type of assessment complain that appraisers apply widely differing meanings to such words, resulting in unfairness and the danger that the whole process falls into disrepute. It should be said that this type of assessment has now largely fallen into disuse because of this difficulty.

The use of objectives as a measure of performance is popular and used by many organisations, often in tandem with a range of performance criteria. An objective is a statement of a result to be achieved within a specified period of time, such as:

• To ensure that accurate monthly returns from the previous month are prepared and distributed to each member of the management team by the sixth working day of each month.

• To review and evaluate producing effective recommendations for the introduction of an alternative system for record keeping by ...

Objectives are personal, to be achieved by one individual unless they are defined as divisional or departmental objectives which are to be cascaded down throughout the organisation. Using objectives alone as a method of assessing performance can create difficulties if an appraiser has to make assessments which require comparison of performance of one person against another.

Many organisations find that the difficulty of setting meaningful objectives for a wide range of people make them less than useful as a measure of performance. Organisations do, however, use objectives to measure performance and we describe below how this can be achieved.

Objectives as a measure of performance

Objectives which are discussed and agreed between the appraiser and the appraisee will always be more effective than objectives which are imposed without discussion and agreement. Of course, at times the appraiser will have to take a lead in devising appropriate objectives. This will be especially true when, as is the case in many organisations, some objectives are cascaded down through the organisation. This happens when each level of the organisation is expected to make their contribution to achieving the corporate objectives at the appropriate level and in the appropriate way. In these cases the appraiser should tell the appraisee in advance what the corporate objectives mean in terms of the accountabilities and responsibilities of the job holder and ask them to think through how these could be expressed as objectives.

When this type of preparation is carried out in advance the discussion at the appraisal interview is much easier to handle and much more focused than if the requirement is introduced for the first time at the interview. Involving people in clarifying and taking a joint approach to setting objectives is always more effective than imposing them. We will return to this subject when we come to the section on how to set objectives.

The starting point for setting objectives has to be an agreed list of the main accountabilities or job requirements. Once both parties are agreed about what the main outputs from the job holder should be, it then remains to consider each one in turn, agreeing standards of performance and targets for each one. In many cases it will not be necessary or appropriate to agree a target in each main area. The important thing is to ensure that targets are set in those areas which are critical to the successful achievement of the main tasks and accountabilities. Generally speaking, it is not advisable to set too many objectives for any one individual; a maximum of six is about what most people can cope with.

Objectives may also be set covering special projects or tasks which the individual is expected to undertake during the appraisal period.

Objective setting in many organisations is less than effective and this can be put down to a small number of reasons, including:

- The objectives set are not critical to the successful achievement of the job accountabilities or main tasks of the job holder. In some cases they are irrelevant and could, if pursued, be a distraction from the main purpose of the job.

- Objectives, once set, are not monitored and quickly fall into disuse.

- The people responsible for setting objectives – appraiser and appraisee – are not sufficiently clear about what an objective is, and lack skills in setting objectives. Therefore, the objectives which are set are inadequate

To overcome these difficulties, organisations need to ensure that adequate training is provided in objective setting. This can often be achieved through on-the-job coaching and need not involve costly training sessions away from the job. If this approach is taken, it is, of course, essential that the coach fully understands objectives and how to set them.

Performance characteristics

The third type of criteria used to measure performance is that of performance characteristics. These are widely used, and while there are some difficulties in devising a perfect set of criteria many organisations consider them to be a useful, practical working tool. The basis for using performance characteristics such as *'knowledge and skills displayed'* as a means of assessing or rating performance requires that a set of characteristics be first of all agreed.

Each organisation must do this for itself as those things which are considered to be important in one organisation may not be as important in another. In practice, many organisations have identified similar sets of characteristics. While it is useful to share and learn from the ideas and experience of others it is not advisable to assume that the basis for assessing performance is transferable. Significant benefit can be derived from a healthy debate within the organisation about which characteristics are most important.

The number of characteristics used can vary, with an average of ten to twelve being used in managerial jobs and a lesser number in clerical or manual jobs. Using a rating scale allows the appraiser to identify low, medium and high performers – information which can then be used as a basis for allocating rewards, if this is what the system requires. Just as importantly though, the rating provides information which the manager/team leader can use in planning improvements in performance and in identifying training needs and needs for on-the-job coaching.

How a rating scale works

A rating scale works by setting out in a list the set of agreed characteristics and applying the appropriate measures. (An example of an appraisal form using a rating scale is shown in Chapter 6.) The measures can be descriptive of the characteristic being assessed, with examples of good, average or poor performance, or the measure can be presented graphically, with the measures being presented as a number of points along a scale.

These lists are normally presented in a format which describes a spectrum from outstanding to unacceptable. A typical scale may include the following:

A – Consistently exceeds performance requirements.

B – Regularly exceeds performance requirements.

C – Meets performance requirements.

D – Fails to meet performance requirements sometimes.

E – Regularly fails to meet performance requirements.

F – Consistently fails to meet performance requirements.

Others express the same basic information as:

A – Outstanding performance.

B – Superior performance.

C – Good performance.

D – Adequate performance.

E – Poor performance.

F – Unacceptable performance.

Another approach is to avoid using descriptive words for each point on the scale and opt for a low score indicator and a high score indicator. The example below refers to a characteristic identified as Task Completion.

Lowest score indicator 1❑ 2❑ 3❑ 4❑ 5❑ 6❑ *Highest score indicator*
Unable to complete tasks/   Consistently completes
assignments within an   tasks/assignments well
acceptable timescale.   within the expected time-
                                                                                  scale.

With this approach the appraiser is left to allocate the appropriate point on the scale with only the low and high indicators as a guide. Many people argue that this system is preferable as any words used as a description carries a value with it which may differ from one individual to another. If, for example, you use the word excellent, the way people interpret it can differ. Using a number scale is less loaded with values, it is claimed.

In constructing scales, organisations need to think about a number of issues.

What will be the impact on an individual who is consistently marked in a negative way? Is it possible to construct a scale which puts a positive perspective on the assessment even though a low rating is being given, for example a low descriptor which states, *'Meets requirements sometimes although there is clear room for improvement'*? This approach avoids using words like satisfactory for the average performers which can be seen as damning with faint praise. It is also usually based on the premise that any unsatisfactory or unacceptable performance must be dealt with at the time it is identified and not left until the appraisal. This means that the scale would be based on four points with the lowest descriptor as indicated above.

What is the most effective number of rating levels? It is generally believed that to have less than three levels from which to choose can result in lowering the reliability of the ratings. Scales from three to six all have their advocates and it is unlikely that one is clearly better than the other. Three and five level scales may lead to a tendency for the appraiser to pull towards the middle. Four and six levels avoid this, with six allowing for more discrimination between the top and bottom performers.

Whatever the scale or number of levels chosen, a key question is how to achieve consistency of marking between appraisers? It is almost inevitable that some appraisers will be perceived as being soft while others will be perceived as being hard. Some appraisers will be accused of treating some individuals as blue eyed boys/girls, while other appraisees will claim they have a personality conflict with the appraiser.

How can these problems be overcome? There is no easy answer to this, which is one of the perennial problems with appraisals.

There are, however, a number of possible ways used by organisations to alleviate the problem if not to resolve it completely:

- *Forced distribution.* Using this system, appraisers are forced to allocate individual marks into a previously agreed distribution. This means that prior to the appraisals being conducted, an expected distribution of scores would be devised, perhaps across the whole organisation or perhaps across individual departments. When all the appraisal forms have been returned the agreed distribution is then applied, moving people at the margins of each level either up or down in order to match the distribution.

Such a distribution on a six level scale, taking 1 as the lowest level score and 6 as the highest level score, could result in the following distribution, which requires 5% of the total population to fall in performance category 1, and so on, for each performance category:

Performance category	*Expected distribution* %
1	5
2	25
3	35
4	20
5	10
6	5

Organisations which have used this approach have found it necessary to skew the distribution away from a normal distribution curve, in order to avoid placing too many employees in the lowest categories. There is also the problem that it creates winners and losers, with some losing out on the basis of a small number of points. Agreeing a cut-off point for the number of people required to enable the distribution to be applied can present difficulty. For example, in a small highly specialised department with perhaps six people it is impossible to apply the distribution, which can only work when applied to large numbers.

The approach is sometimes used as a means of checking the health of the process once all of the appraisals have been completed, when the distribution can be applied to the whole organisation and lessons for the future drawn.

- *A ranking system.* This approach requires all staff to be ranked in order of merit and then for the ratings to be distributed through the rank order. This can and does work for some organisations although it still has to rely on the appraisers making the ratings as objective as possible in the first place.

- *Monitoring and evaluating the process.* A useful way of helping to ensure fairness is for the organisation to be seen to demonstrate that it is concerned to make sure that the system is fair. When senior management is seen to take an active interest, other appraisers are more likely to devote time and attention to getting it right. The monitoring process also involves each appraisal being seen and signed off by the appraiser's manager, often described as the '*grandparent system*', where the more senior manager has an opportunity to review the quality and consistency of the appraisals. In most cases the 'grandparent' will be seeing the appraisals of more then one appraiser and will be able, therefore, to form an opinion about consistency and can take corrective action if necessary. This approach can be further supported by the personnel or human resource department, providing statistics for managers showing the companywide distribution and by providing support and assistance to appraisers during the process. Care must be taken to ensure that this involvement does not lead to ownership of the process being taken away from line management.

- *Training for appraisers and appraisees.* The effective training of all appraisers is an essential part of helping to ensure consistency of marking. If the same messages have been communicated to all appraisers, they are much more likely to conduct the assessments in a similar way. Training needs to reach beyond the initial launch into reviewing the process, sharing the learning and building on the experience of all. Regular training can greatly improve the consistency and fairness of appraisers.

All of these actions can help. However, the one thing above all else which is important is the general climate and atmosphere which surrounds the appraisal process. Is it perceived as a means of management exerting control or is it about a genuine desire to improve the contribution and performance of all through openness, honesty and feedback? A process which is seeking to build on the strengths of the high performers and through development and coaching to help bring up the performance level of the less than effective performers will always be more effective.

Management style is an important part of ensuring the success of an appraisal system. An open empowering style is more likely to lead to a successful appraisal process than a closed controlling style.

The frequency of appraisal

Most appraisals take place once a year, with some organisations using a process which requires appraisers to hold a formal interview twice each year. Taking the once a year appraisal as the norm, many organisations supplement this with a shorter interim appraisal which is held three times in the year. This approach requires each manager/team leader to put some time aside to speak personally to each member of their team four times each year. When put in this way, most people would agree that it is not an onerous task.

When an interim appraisal is conducted, the appraiser is often asked to complete a much shorter review form and keep it on file for reference, especially at the main appraisal. In these instances the review does not generally involve anyone except the appraiser and appraisee, with the 'grandparent' being involved if required.

Interim appraisals provide a useful opportunity to review progress with development activities which have been agreed and to review and update objectives in the light of changing circumstances. One of the realities in today's world of work is the constant change we all experience – at times this leads to previously agreed objectives becoming out of date before they are achieved. Interim appraisal allows the review and change, if necessary, to take place with the minimum of fuss.

As has already been mentioned above, some organisations separate the performance review element of appraisal from the developmental element. There are strong arguments in favour of this approach – some people may feel constrained talking about development and prospects when their performance is under review. Others feel that recent performance can play too large a part in the appraiser's mind when considering potential and it would be disingenuous to suggest that a manager's views on potential are never influenced by recent performance. Yet it is well known that people who perform poorly in one role and sometimes with one manager can, with the right help, encouragement and challenge, deliver outstanding performance in a different role.

When designing a new appraisal system or reviewing an existing one, consideration should be given to the possibility of separating the two elements.

Perhaps the most important thing to say about the frequency of appraisal is that appraising and seeking to improve the performance of team members is a constant and ongoing responsibility of all managers/team leaders. An annual, twice yearly or interim appraisal provides an opportunity to do this in a slightly more formal and structured way. It should not, however, be used as an excuse for failing to constantly appraise the performance of team members.

Chapter 3

THE APPRAISER

WHO SHOULD APPRAISE?

In the past this question would not have been asked – it would have been taken for granted that the only person who should appraise another in any organisation was someone more senior than the person being appraised. Happily this is no longer the case and we are seeing a whole new approach to appraisal in many organisations. This new approach involves extending the range of people who appraise others.

It is increasingly popular to talk about involving more people in appraisal. What this means in practice will differ from one organisation to another, but generally it is taken to mean appraisal by a manager/team leader, self-appraisal, appraisal by peers, upward appraisal and appraisal by customers, although in most cases appraisal by customers usually means the internal customer. Many more people are looking at how they can improve their appraisal systems through drawing information and feedback from a wider range of interested parties.

The processes involved in consulting more people can be complex and as the range of involvement extends it will be important to make sure that the outcome is not just an extension of a bigger, more time consuming and more cumbersome bureaucracy. Ideally, the outcome should be a more effective and informative process of reviewing performance, providing feedback and improving performance.

We will look at each of the possible appraisers in turn and the contribution they can make to improving the effectiveness of appraisal.

MANAGEMENT APPRAISAL

Traditionally, the only appraiser would be either the direct manager of the individual or the manager's manager, generally referred to as the 'grandparent'. The process would be that the manager would receive the appraisal form, complete it, and agree the assessments given with their own manager.

The manager would then conduct the interview during which the lead role would clearly be taken by the manager. The manager would be responsible for driving the process, the whole process being seen as providing the manager with an opportunity to **tell** the appraisee how he or she was doing.

In some cases the process would involve the immediate manager of the appraisee in preparing the form and then passing it to the 'grandparent', who would conduct the appraisal interview.

In most organisations both of these approaches, which were characteristic of a much more formal age and management style, have long gone. More typically nowadays the process has been opened up into an affair which involves the appraisee in playing a full role with the interview becoming a two-way, rather than a one-way, process.

As organisations change, with fewer layers of management and in many cases with managers having more direct reports and more people working on projects rather than in permanent teams, it will become increasingly more difficult for managers to conduct appraisals in the traditional way. The manager may have too many direct reports to be able to appraise them effectively; in some cases managers may have a shared responsibility for people and have difficulty in agreeing who should appraise who. It is even possible to envisage a situation where a manager does not see some direct reports often enough to be able to adequately appraise them.

The response to such changes has to be flexible and open, seeking new ways to achieve effective appraisal. Of course, it also needs to be said that for many organisations the scenario outlined above is still a long way from reality. It is important not to assume that a few progressive organisations in markets which may have changed radically should be the benchmark against which others should be compared. The key for each organisation is to review the specific needs they face and constantly keep under review their existing system with a view to introducing changes as appropriate.

For most organisations, into the foreseeable future, immediate managers will continue to play an important part in the appraisals of their reports.

SELF-APPRAISAL

Self-appraisal is not a recent innovation, having been around in some organisations for many years. For many individuals it is as much a part of appraisal as that conducted by the manager. Very few, if any, organisations which have included self-appraisal as part of their process would wish to go back to a manager only appraisal system.

The idea of self-appraisal is very much in tune with many of the other current developments in management style which we have seen in recent years, such as empowerment and expecting all employees to take a much greater responsibility for what they do. It is reasonably argued that as organisations expect people to accept more responsibility for their work they should also accept that each individual should have an opportunity to participate in their own appraisal.

Any debate about self-appraisal should not be about whether to include it as part of the appraisal system, but about the most effective method of including it.

The way to include it varies with the type of system which is in use. Some organisations produce a separate form for self-appraisal, while others include a specific section on the form the manager uses and the manager then gives each individual a photocopy of the form to complete before the interview. The second approach is more widely used when some form of rating is called for. A further variation applies when the setting and assessing of objectives is the main basis for the appraisal. Each of these variations will be considered in turn before looking at self-appraisal in general.

The use of a separate form

A special form for self-appraisal is given to each employee who has to complete it before the appraisal interview. If such a form is used it will usually set out a number of questions which ask the individual to rate themselves on how well they have performed across a wide range of areas. Such questions are generally open-ended and designed to stimulate thinking as well as attempting to assess performance. The questions may well include a selection of the following, although it is unlikely that any system would include as many as is given below:

- Which parts of your job have you performed well in since the last review?

- Which of your achievements have you been most pleased with?

- What, if any, problems have you had with your work since the last review?

- Did you achieve all of your objectives in a satisfactory manner?

- Is there anything you could have done better?

- Have you experienced any difficulty in meeting the performance standards for your job?

- Do you know enough about what is expected of you?

- Are there any areas of your job where your performance could be improved?

- Have you any ideas about how this improvement could be achieved?

- Do you enjoy your job? Is it too easy? Too difficult?

- Do you need to acquire any further skills or knowledge to help you do your job more effectively? For other reasons? List any suggestions you want to make.

- What objectives would you set for yourself for the next period?

- What personal development plans will you make for yourself for the next period?

In some cases the answers to these questions would be given to the appraiser before the appraisal meeting and they would then form part of the agenda for the discussion. This approach encourages the appraisee to take a lead in the appraisal discussion, leaving the appraiser to respond and provide help in the most appropriate way.

An appraiser in responding to a self-appraisal should take care not to get involved in a confrontation with the appraisee and has to ensure that they remain focused on the issues, not on the person. This approach, however, does not mean that the appraiser should accept the assessment the individual makes without question. The element of self-appraisal is designed to provide greater involvement for the appraisee in the process, it is not the appraisal. The appraisal has to be a joint discussion between the two parties.

20

Using a rating scale

With this type of system it is likely that the appraisee will use the same form as the appraiser. The way it works is that the appraiser will give the appraisee a photocopy of the form and ask the appraisee to complete the self-appraisal element in the appropriate boxes and return it to the appraiser before the interview.

The example of the appraisal using a rating scale given in Chapter 2 is repeated below showing how this form could be adapted to include self-appraisal.

Lowest score indicator 1☐ 2☐ 3☐ 4☐ 5☐ 6☐   *Highest score indicator*
Unable to complete tasks/   Consistently completes
assignments within an   tasks/assignments well
acceptable timescale.   within the expected time-
                                                             scale.

Self-Appraisal Mark ☐

Using this system, the appraisee would place a score for each element on the scale in the box indicated before giving the form back to the appraiser. The appraiser would then make an assessment and score each element. In many cases the appraiser would be asked to make the initial score in pencil indicating that it was open to change as a result of the discussion.

The appraisal interview would then take place with the objective being to seek agreement on the ratings each had given.

Setting and assessing objectives

This type of system is based wholly on the setting and achievement of objectives. The individual's performance is judged on how well they achieved the objectives which had been set for the period. It is not hard to imagine that in order for the system to work effectively, a great deal of attention and skill is required in setting objectives.

The self-appraisal element requires that the appraisee review the objectives for the previous period and assess how far they have been achieved. The appraiser does likewise, and the discussion centres around the reasons for achievement or not.

Difficulties with self-appraisal

Self-appraisal encourages employees to play a full part in assessing their own performance, and as such is a good progressive step for organisations to take. The effectiveness of the approach does, however, depend on a number of other factors, not least of which is the general atmosphere regarding responsibility and empowerment.

If the generally perceived style of management is one of control rather than empowerment, it should come as no surprise that introducing self-appraisal will be treated with suspicion and distrust. In an organisation seeking to move from a controlling management style, to a more open style, self-appraisal may be an appropriate part of that shift, but if it is the only evidence of that shift, it may be best not to introduce it until other changes in the atmosphere and culture of the organisation have been seen to take place.

Self-appraisal requires much greater skill in appraisal interviewing. When all the manager had to do was complete an appraisal for an individual and tell them what was in it, control remained firmly with the manager. As soon as the individual is involved in appraising themselves, a whole new set of issues is opened up for the manager. What if the manager disagrees with the self-assessment? What if the appraisee disagrees with the manager's rating? Who has the final say on what the mark will be?

Dealing with this situation demands great skill in persuasion, in negotiation and in handling conflict, to say nothing of the skill required in being able to give and receive both negative and positive feedback.

Research seems to suggest that when individuals conduct a self-appraisal they are likely to assess themselves realistically and not rate their achievements so highly as to create a problem for the manager. This, however, may not be the case if a rating scale is being used, and the rating has a direct relationship to some form of performance related pay – in such cases they are unlikely to underscore their achievements. Personal experience in a number of organisations and anecdotal evidence from others suggests that while self-appraisal seldom leads to an individual making a wholly unrealistic assessment of their performance, where a rating scale is used it does lead to some element of marking up. This approach is often the result of the appraisee taking up a negotiating or bargaining position which, in time-honoured fashion, is always set a little above what you realistically expect to achieve.

Coping with this and coming out with a realistic agreed assessment and a motivated employee requires a great deal of management skill. In many ways this goes back to the question of openness and trust referred to earlier, and in an organisation where this exists, there is less likely to be a problem.

A further issue – and one which exercises some employees greatly – is whether the self-appraisal should be given to the appraiser before the appraisal interview. In most organisations this practice is the one which is followed but some employees may feel inhibited by having to commit themselves in advance. The problem, however, is one of openness and trust, and on balance I believe that if the appraisal is to be seen as essentially a helping opportunity rather than an opportunity for criticism, the more information the appraiser has the better.

Making self-appraisal work

Each organisation will have to identify the specific difficulties and barriers it will have to overcome in making self-appraisal work. However, there are a few key things which, if done well, will greatly help:

- Self-appraisal works best in an environment where trust and openness thrive all the year round. If appraisal is an annual event and is seen as the only time when employees are expected to contribute and comment on performance, it is less likely to work and may create more problems than it solves.

- Self-appraisal has to be supported by an effective communications programme aimed at all employees. Such a programme should explain fully the process and allow ample time and opportunity for employees to ask questions and raise concerns. These questions and concerns should always be answered fully and sympathetically.

- A communications programme which supported the introduction of the system some years ago will have been forgotten and needs to be renewed.

- Appraisers need to be well trained in the whole process and especially in interviewing skills. Organisations which stint on the training of appraisers are asking for trouble.

- Appraisers and appraisees should be trained in giving and receiving feedback and joint problem-solving skills.

- The whole appraisal – and especially the self-appraisal element – should be seen as motivational and performance improving, looking to the future rather than the past.

Peer appraisal

With greater emphasis being placed on teamworking as a means of improving performance, it is inevitable that more organisations will want to use peer assessments as part of the appraisal process. The approach is already in use in some organisations. This form of assessment is, of course, likely to work more effectively in an organisation which already has a strong team-based culture. Providing the emphasis is positive and seeks to establish ways in which performance can be improved, it can work very effectively.

The process usually requires the assistance of someone external to the team – frequently a representative from the personnel or human resource department – to act as a facilitator, although some organisations use specially trained facilitators from other parts of the organisation to help with the process.

Questionnaires are issued to all team members, who are asked to complete them anonymously and return them to the facilitator.

Feedback is then given to the individuals and the team leader. This can be done individually in private, or it can be done openly at a team meeting where everyone receives their individual feedback personally and then has an opportunity to discuss it with the other team members. If it is to be done at a team meeting it is essential to have a trained facilitator available to assist the process and to help keep the discussion on the issues rather than the people.

The facilitator in analysing all the questionnaires identifies those issues which seem to be getting in the way of improved performance. At the open discussion and feedback attention would be focused on how to resolve these issues in developing a plan for the future.

In addition to this, some individuals may need some personal counselling or coaching on some of the results of the questionnaires referring to them. In most cases this will be best handled privately by either the team leader or the facilitator.

The type of questions which can be included in peer assessment questionnaires generally cover team-based behaviour, and may involve peers being asked to comment on:

- How cooperative and helpful is X?

- How well does X contribute to team activities?

- How would you rate X as a team member who contributes to the success of the team?

- How does X maintain effective relationships with other team members?

- How does X contribute to team morale?

- What actions could X take to improve their performance and the performance of the team?

As will be appreciated, such questions raise sensitive issues which need careful handling. This is why peer assessment should always be supported by trained help from outside the team. The comments regarding openness and trust made above about self-appraisal apply with equal force to peer appraisal.

Difficulties with peer appraisal

An effective process of peer appraisal based on teams can contribute significantly to the success of the teams; badly handled, it can cause rather than solve problems. The involvement of a trained facilitator to assist feedback between team members can help to ensure the success of the process.

Great care needs to be taken with the design of the questionnaire to ensure that it is easily understood and easily completed. Poorly phrased questions and a badly designed questionnaire can result in the expression of distortion and prejudice rather than an emphasis on positive reasons for improvement and change.

It must be ensured that the process does not become a popularity poll within the team which can be influenced by the personality of some team members rather than the contribution they make.

The process requires a lot of administrative support and can easily become too bureaucratic and time consuming. Care should be taken that the effort required to make the system work does not outweigh the benefits gained.

Attention should be paid to the role of the manager/team leader in the process. They must be fully involved in the process and not feel that this new process is taking away their responsibility for appraising their people.

Making peer appraisal work

All that was said above under this heading in the section on self-appraisal applies with equal force in terms of peer appraisal. In addition one other thing should be noted.

- **A process of peer appraisal should never be introduced across the whole organisation unless a well monitored pilot scheme has been tried first, assessed and amended as necessary.**

UPWARD APPRAISAL

There is little doubt that with the organisational climate which is opening up, upward appraisal will become increasingly popular in the future. In application it is similar to peer appraisal and many of the same difficulties are likely to be encountered.

The process requires the design of some clearly defined objectives for what **you** want to achieve out of the introduction of a process of upward appraisal – mostly this is to ask team members to comment on particular aspects of their manager's performance. In particular people are asked to comment on those aspects of the performance which have a direct relevance to the performance of the team members. Once the objectives have been agreed, you can then go on to design an appropriate system and questionnaire. The aim is to provide some feedback to the manager from the perspective of the team member.

Once the questionnaire has been agreed it will be given to each person who reports to the particular manager/team leader. Questionnaires are usually completed anonymously and returned to a central place, usually the personnel or human resource department for analysis. While the questionnaire should be completed anonymously, the name of the individual being appraised should be clearly stated to avoid any confusion if a lot of questionnaires are being returned at the same time.

There are a number of organisations who offer computer-based systems with ready-made questionnaires designed to appraise managers and team leaders. Most will amend the questionnaires to include specific questions covering areas you want to cover if they are not already included.

These same companies also include in the package the analysis and preparation of results ready for feedback to the manager/team leader. Using this approach reduces much of the time-consuming hassle and administration. It ensures complete privacy as the results are analysed off site; however, it does also reduce the flexibility you have in operating the system. The design of the system should be driven by what you want to achieve and about how best to achieve it. If you decide to opt for external assistance you should, of course, shop around for the system and organisation most likely to suit your needs.

Upward appraisal questionnaires will usually present the questions on a scale to allow for different responses. An example might be:

	Very rarely				*Almost always*	
Communicates regularly	1 ❑	2 ❑	3 ❑	4 ❑	5 ❑	6 ❑

A further refinement can be to ask how important the employee feels the particular behaviour is. So the question could appear as:

Not		*Very*				*Very*			*Almost*
important		*important*				*rarely*			*always*
1 ❑	2 ❑	3 ❑	4 ❑	Communicates regularly		1 ❑	2 ❑	3 ❑	4 ❑

The analysis can then allow for an average and a high and low score, in terms of how important the appraisers see the behaviour and how regularly they perceive the appraisee as demonstrating it.

Most questionnaires are concerned with gaining feedback about clearly defined behaviours, such as how often the appraisee communicates, rather than the more subjective issues like leadership, although where an issue like leadership can be expressed in a measurable way it could be included. It is important to remember that this type of appraisal can only ask about how people perceive the individual, so the inclusion of some questions about how the appraisers perceive a particular behaviour may be valid. When looking at the following list of questions it is important to remember that the appraisee in this case is the manager.

Questions usually cover issues like:

* How supportive and helpful is the appraisee to the reports?
* How good is the appraisee at giving feedback?
* Does the appraisee delegate effectively?
* Does the appraisee inspire trust and confidence?
* Does the appraisee behave in an empowering way?
* Is the appraisee always available to provide help and guidance when required?
* Does the appraisee make decisions quickly and effectively?

Clearly, there are numerous issues which could be covered and which ones you choose will depend on what you are seeking to achieve. It is important, however, not to include too many – a minimum of eight and a maximum of twelve is about the right target.

Once the results have been analysed and results are available, you need to decide how to handle the question of feedback. This is usually handled in a face-to-face meeting with the appraisee and a trained facilitator. Some organisations have opted to follow this with an open team meeting, with a facilitator taking the lead, where the emphasis is on change and performance improvement. How to provide the feedback is a sensitive issue and should be handled as such, the involvement of a trained facilitator external to the team being essential.

Difficulties with upward appraisal

All that was said above about peer appraisal applies with equal force to upward appraisal. It is a very powerful tool and as such it is essential to get it right. If it is handled badly it can create real problems for all parties – the team member, the manager and the organisation.

Making upward appraisal work

The guidelines given in the section on self-appraisal should be followed and a pilot scheme should always be carried out before a system of upward appraisal is introduced across an organisation.

Perhaps it is not appropriate or necessary to conduct an upward appraisal for every manager/ team leader every year. The danger of building a bureaucracy for what may be a marginal return should perhaps point us towards doing this type of appraisal every two or three years.

THE FUTURE

Organisations are increasingly recognising that the traditional approach to appraisal where a manager appraises subordinates is inadequate – it may be better than no appraisal at all, but it is not good enough for meeting the future requirements of many organisations. In this chapter we have looked at management appraisal, self-appraisal, peer appraisal and upward appraisal. All of these are in existence in many organisations and growing in use. Building on this, and in response to the demand for a continuous improvement in performance, some organisations have started to look for a wider range of appraisers.

These now include all of those mentioned above, and in a growing number of cases customers, both external and internal, and colleagues who are not part of the same team but who may have a dependency on the appraisee. To support this – and in order to reduce the bureaucracy and the potential administrative nightmare which would be required to conduct appraisals on this scale – some organisations have developed a system of 360 degree appraisal. This all-round appraisal is usually supported by computer-based analysis and results production, either developed in-house or bought externally, and can provide a lot of information in a manageable format.

The future will undoubtedly see a growth in the use of this type of extended appraisal in different forms and for different reasons in response to the requirements of different organisations.

If your appraisal system is still based around a manager appraising a subordinate, it is in urgent need of a thorough overhaul. If your appraisal system has been in place for five years or more without a full-scale review, now is the time to conduct a review. Few, if any, appraisal systems are robust enough to last for longer than five years without an overhaul.

Chapter 4

THE MAIN COMPONENTS OF AN APPRAISAL SYSTEM

HOW THE PROCESS WORKS

The majority of appraisal systems include a number of elements which together help the system to work and meet the objectives set for it. As has been said before, how effectively these objectives are achieved will depend more on how people use the system than on what the system consists of. Most systems, however, follow a similar format which covers:

- a review of performance;

- setting objectives for the next period;

- assessment of potential;

- personal development plans;

- summary and agreement;

- sign off;

- additional comments made by the 'grandparent';

- administration.

We will look at each of these stages in turn.

A review of performance

A primary purpose of appraisal is to seek ways of improving individual and team performance and therefore it should come as no surprise that the starting point for most appraisal systems is a review of performance. Such a review will usually start with both parties looking back over the period since the last review and exploring the performance of the appraisee.

This process may be helped by the appraisee having completed some form of self-appraisal before the appraisal interview. It certainly requires the appraiser to have done some preparation and made an assessment of the performance of the appraisee. The process works best if the appraiser is able to identify specific examples of good performance and aspects of performance which could be improved. If specific examples are not available it is much more difficult to focus the discussion and plan for improvement.

An important element at this stage – and in fact at all stages of the appraisal interview – is that there should be no surprises. In other words, the appraiser should not raise any critical issues which have not been discussed with the appraisee before. An appraisal is not the one time in the year when a manager has the opportunity to tell an individual that they need to improve their performance. Such discussion and feedback should be part of the regular manager/employee interchange.

The effective appraiser will, during the review period, have noted aspects of performance which are appropriate to raise for discussion at the appraisal meeting. Some of these may provide opportunities for praise, while others may be aspects of performance which could be improved. If they are significant, they should have been discussed with the appraisee at the time they were noticed.

Even during the appraisal discussion, self-appraisal plays an important part and the appraiser should be asking questions such as, *'What do you consider to have been your strongest points during the last period?'* Or, *'In which areas would you like to be looking to improve your performance?'* This approach leaves the responsibility clearly in the hands of the appraisee, rather than allowing the appraiser to fall into the trap of doing the telling. We will return to this subject when we consider the performance review interview in Chapter 9 of this report.

The objective and purpose of the review of performance is to have an open and honest discussion about past performance with a view to seeking opportunities for improvement.

Setting objectives for the next period

Even if the setting and achievement of objectives is not to play a major part in the system being operated, the appraiser and appraisee will find it useful to discuss possible improvements in performance as targets to aim for. This approach will help to focus the minds of both parties on the need for measuring outcomes, *'If we agree that you will seek to improve your performance on x during the next period, how will we know when you have succeeded?'*

The review of performance provides an ideal platform on which to build targets and objectives for the next period. This discussion should flow naturally from opportunities for improvement to the more specific: this is what we will do and this is how we will measure success.

If the setting of objectives is a formal part of the process, it follows naturally from the review of performance and the assessment of how well the objectives for the previous period have been achieved to move into a discussion of objectives for the next period.

Assessment of potential

Many appraisal systems require the appraiser to make some form of judgement about the potential or promotability of the appraisee. This is frequently on a simple scale which requires the appraiser to indicate the level the appraisee could be expected to reach in a given number of years. There are many difficulties with this, and, not surprisingly, many managers find it difficult to assess the suitability of the appraisee in terms of their potential to progress to a level above that which the assessor currently occupies.

A more legitimate and appropriate expectation may be to ask the appraiser to give some indication of if and when the appraisee will be ready and equipped to move on to the position above the one the appraisee currently occupies.

If the system requires the appraiser to make an assessment about potential or promotability it usually takes place at this stage in the discussion, after the review of performance and discussion of objectives.

We will return to this issue in more detail in Chapter 8.

Personal development plans

All appraisals should include a section where the individual has an opportunity to express their desires and aspirations for the future. As has already been mentioned, some organisations consider this to be such an essential part of the process that they have separated it from the review of performance and encourage a special discussion to concentrate on development issues. If this is not the case it is essential that the appraiser allows sufficient time for an adequate discussion about aspirations, and plans for achieving them.

It is sad to say that in far too many appraisal discussions this element is neglected and can even be omitted entirely. On other occasions it is treated as though an individual's future aspirations can be boiled down to the simple question, *'Which course would you like to go on next year?'*

A discussion about aspirations and plans for achieving them, the training needs they throw up and how they will be met is an essential part of appraisal. Additionally, the appraiser may have identified a training need which may help to overcome a shortfall in performance. This may require some discussion and should be placed on the agenda. The appraisee should be asked to consider aspirations, development plans and training during preparation for the meeting and should be encouraged to take the lead and the ownership for the outcomes from this part of the appraisal.

Summary and agreement

Most appraisal discussions cover a lot of ground in a short period of time and some significant decisions and plans can be made. It is important, therefore, to make sure that all of these are captured and agreed. The most effective way of doing this is to summarise at the end of each main stage of the appraisal discussion and also to include a final summary before the end. This should seek to ensure that both parties leave the discussion with clear agreement about what each is going to do.

Where clear objectives for future action have been agreed, it may be appropriate to put them in writing after the meeting so that both parties have a record of them.

Sign off

It has always been a traditional part of the appraisal process that both parties sign the final document at the end of the meeting. In some cases this was introduced to ensure that the manager did actually show the appraisal to the individual. This was considered to be necessary especially when a system was undergoing a change from a closed to a more open approach. Perhaps in the past the manager had not been required to show the form to the individual being appraised, or even hold a discussion with them. When a new system was introduced requiring the manager to show the form to the individual some form of proof was required to ensure that this was done.

Nowadays, however, it has become the accepted norm that each individual should sign their appraisal form to indicate that they have seen the contents. Much discussion in some organisations surrounds the issue of whether or not signing the form signifies agreement with all that is contained on the form. In order to overcome this problem the employee who wishes to signal disagreement is usually allowed to sign the form and add, 'Seen but not agreed.'

Where objectives have been agreed they are often written on the appraisal form, so it becomes doubly important for both parties to sign to signify that they agree with the objectives which have been set.

Additional comments made by the 'grandparent'

Most systems allow for some oversight of the appraisal by the manager's manager or 'grandparent'. This is to ensure that information on performance is passed up the line to help with ensuring fairness and equity across a wider spectrum and to provide more senior people with insights into the performance, potential and aspirations of people who report to them indirectly.

A contentious issue arises when the more senior manager not only sees the form but has the opportunity to make comments. The issue is, does the appraisee have an opportunity to see these comments? Moreover, if, as a consequence, the appraisee does not agree with the comments, what action is then available?

Experience suggests that where these additional comments have direct impact on pay, bonus, grading or promotion, then the individual should have an opportunity to have the comments and possible outcomes explained. Where the comments do not have any direct impact they are frequently not made available to the appraisee. This of course poses ethical questions if the organisation claims to have an open system.

The danger, as can be imagined, is that the whole process can become a never ending cycle of meeting and signing. A solution some organisations adopt to avoid this is that the more senior manager only comments by exception and these comments are always conveyed back to the employee. If they impact directly on pay, the employee can disagree and challenge them through any appeals procedure which exists.

The most effective way of involving the more senior manager is to involve them at an earlier stage in the process – in other words, before the appraisal interviews take place. This way they can have a real input into the question of fairness and equity across all of the reports.

Administration

Central administration of the system is essential if the process is going to work across the whole organisation. The secret, however, is not letting administration become ownership. As indicated in Chapter 1, if a system is to be relevant to and focused on improving performance, it must be owned by the line managers.

Central administration, however, is required to fulfil a number of functions:

- To issue the appraisal forms at the appropriate time.

- To make sure that everyone is fully informed about their role in appraisal through the design and delivery of appropriate communications and training.

- To collect and analyse the data for organisational use at the end of the period, including identification of training needs and data required for succession planning.

- To hold on file the completed appraisal forms for future use in assisting promotion and appointment decisions if required.

- To provide an overall view, and, as far as possible, to ensure that the process is fair and equitable across the organisation as a whole.

- To administer an appeals procedure if one is required.

- To keep under review the effectiveness and relevance of the system, suggesting and introducing improvements as necessary.

Each of these functions is necessary to ensure that the process of appraisal is effective. The danger to watch for is when the central administration becomes too bureaucratic, and the emphasis of the process shifts from a clear focus on improving performance at a local level to fulfilling the needs of the central administration. When this happens, line managers should pull the ownership back to where it belongs.

Chapter 5

HOW AN APPRAISAL SYSTEM OPERATES

SHOULD IT COVER THE WHOLE ORGANISATION?

Some appraisal systems have grown up piecemeal. For example, the sales director believes that appraisal would be a good thing for his part of the organisation and introduces it. Then other people become aware of the benefits and follow suit, or in some cases even introduce a different system. Nowadays, however, it is much more usual for an organisation to design and introduce a system which applies across all departments.

Organisations are much more interdependent than they used to be and this implies that an integrated system is more likely to meet the needs of the majority. In those organisations which use a rating scale to assess performance, some have introduced a weighting to the scale which can be applied differently to some sections or divisions. If this is necessary to ensure relevance and local ownership, the results are likely to be beneficial. If, however, it is done at the whim of a powerful manager it can be seen as divisive and should be avoided.

For most organisations it should be possible to design a system which can be applied equally across the whole.

Does it need to cover the whole organisation to work?

Ideally, of course, the whole organisation should be concerned to assess and seek to improve performance; however, this is not always realistic for a variety of reasons. So, in the absence of a system covering the whole organisation, it is perfectly possible to design a system for a part of an organisation.

The process involved should not differ from that which would apply to a system for the whole organisation; all of the same opportunities and pitfalls are likely to be present and will need to be taken into account.

Given that the requirements of such a system are likely to be much more localised or at least directed at a particular business unit does not mean that the unit concerned can afford to skimp on issues such as communications and training. As much care for these elements must be taken as with a system covering the whole organisation.

A LINK TO PAY?

Many appraisal systems have a direct link to pay, though in some cases – hopefully a small minority – the view is taken that the only purpose of appraisal is to determine pay. This view unfortunately is to sadly misunderstand the real benefit which appraisal can bring to an organisation and – more importantly – to the individual manager and employee. Where there is a direct link to pay, great care has to be taken to ensure that this does not dominate the whole of the appraisal system. As has been mentioned in Chapter 1 of this report, some organisations have separated the assessment of performance and the personal development aspects of appraisal in order to avoid this happening.

Clearly, where an organisation uses a process of performance related pay (PRP), there has to be some means of assessing performance and the appraisal system is a logical – although not the only – way. In some cases a quite separate assessment is made in relation to pay, although whether employees see this distinction is another matter.

The issue of performance related pay is highly controversial with strong arguments in favour and against. Much has been written on the subject and it is not appropriate to review the whole debate here. It is, however, worth considering briefly, why organisations introduce PRP.

The objectives are generally straightforward and are likely to include:

- To make a positive statement about the commitment of the organisation to high levels of performance.

- To provide additional motivation for employees, through enabling them to achieve significant increases in pay.

- To reward people according to the contribution they make.

- To provide a clear distinction between the rewards received by the high performers and the less than good.

- To raise performance across the organisation.

- To reinforce a process of culture change.

- To support the wider introduction of a system of performance management.

- To help recruit and retain key high performing employees.

Unfortunately these positive reasons don't always get across to employees who frequently seem to believe that the main purpose of PRP is to cut the pay bill.

People who favour PRP frequently argue that it is an effective means of motivating employees. However, what evidence is available actually suggests that this is a very open question, with the majority believing that while pay may act as a short-term motivator, the effect of it does not carry over the longer term.

It has to be said that the introduction of PRP in many organisations has been less than successful, although in others, where perhaps the expectation of what it would deliver was more realistic, more success has been achieved. It is not a panacea, a means of curing all ills, and on its own it will not lead to significant improvements in performance. As part of a structured and planned process of culture change and linked with other key elements of performance management, it can, undoubtedly, work for some organisations.

When making decisions about the introduction of an appraisal system for the first time or when undertaking a major overhaul of an existing system, an important consideration will be whether or not to include a direct link to pay. This is not something which organisations can afford to shirk; equally, however, the direct link with pay is not something which should be automatically included. It is an important issue and should be debated fully during the development process, and especially when thinking about the aims and objectives for the system. If you are clear about what you are trying to achieve, the design of the system and whether or not to include pay as part of the process becomes much easier.

COMMUNICATIONS

The appraisal meeting itself is an excellent opportunity for open and honest communication between manager and employee. It will not work effectively, however, unless it has been preceded and supported by a communications programme covering the whole process. It is unfortunately true that some organisations fail to understand the importance of communications and give this issue less attention than it requires.

Effective communication is required at all levels, to all managers and employees. It should start early on in the process, informing people that an appraisal system is going to be introduced. This should be followed as soon as possible with more specific information such as the aims and objectives and as much of the process as has been agreed and can reasonably be discussed at this stage. During the development phase representative samples of managers should be consulted along with employee representatives – this consultation in itself is a form of communication.

When the details of the system have been agreed they should be communicated to all employees as soon as possible. The programme of communication outlined below is provided as a model for organisations to follow: it sets out the essential elements of a communication process.

The programme is designed to start once the basic details of the appraisal system which is going to be introduced have been agreed. The aims, the objectives, the appraisal forms to be used and the process to be followed will all have been agreed and approved before the start of the communications programme.

Phase one

This is essentially the preparatory phase and is concerned with broad information and identifying concerns which will need to be taken account of.

- The company magazine is a useful starting point and an article covering the detail of the process, and giving a timetable of events, can help to focus the thinking of all.

- Following the article face-to-face briefing sessions for all managers and employees should be held at which the process can be outlined and questions answered. At this stage managers and employees can attend the same session, unless there are some specific messages which are to be communicated to managers only, although it should be noted that further training/briefing sessions will be held later to deal with the specifics.

- The briefing sessions and questions will have provided a lot of useful information regarding concerns and uncertainties which can now be considered and dealt with.

Phase two

This is the phase which leads up to the introduction of the appraisal meetings and should be timed to be as close as possible to the dates when the appraisals will be held. Clearly, this will be influenced by the numbers to be trained and briefed.

- Two written guides will be required, one for all employees and one for appraisers. Both guides should contain as much detail as necessary to give everyone a good understanding of the system and process – what will happen, how it will happen, and if possible when it will happen. Some organisations include in the employees' guide a series of questions and answers, covering the main concerns raised at the first briefing. The appraisers' guide should explain the role of the appraiser: what they have to do before, during and after the appraisal interview. It will also explain how to complete the appraisal form.

- **All** appraisers, no matter how experienced or at what level they are, should receive training. An outline programme covering the detail of a proposed training programme is given in Chapter 10. Training is a key part of the overall communications programme.

- Training, briefing and information giving are also essential for all of those to be appraised. The same amount of time is not required and they can be carried out in much larger groups, but they cannot be missed. Further detail is given in Chapter 11. They can only be done effectively face-to-face, with ample opportunity for question and discussion.

- Some organisations find that at this stage it is also useful to provide some special briefing or training for employee representatives. In some cases the full course for appraisers is provided for this group. This helps to allay fears and concerns, and provides a useful opportunity for debate and discussion.

- At each of these training/briefing sessions copies of the appropriate guides should be given to all participants. Copies of the appraisal form to be used should also be provided and discussed. Clearly, key elements of the process such as self-appraisal and objective setting will need to be explained in detail.

Phase three

This phase is more concerned with the role of the appraiser and includes the appraisal meeting.

- Prior to the appraisal meeting each appraiser should hold a short briefing session for all of their appraisees. At this briefing it is useful to outline the process again, what will happen and when, discuss personal expectations and encourage all to complete the self-appraisal. The appraiser should also state their expectations and demonstrate enthusiasm for the process.

- The appraisal meeting should take place soon after the briefing – how soon, will, of course, depend on the number of people to be appraised. This stage is outlined fully in Chapter 9.

- Communication does not end once the interview has been completed. It is necessary for the appraiser to keep people informed about the follow-up actions which have been agreed.

In many ways, the success of a new appraisal system is as dependent on the way it is communicated as on the effectiveness of the system itself. It is to be expected that in an organisation which does not have a tradition of formal appraisal, the introduction of appraisal will be treated with a degree of suspicion. This can only be overcome by open and effective communication.

HANDLING DISAGREEMENTS

Experience suggests that serious disagreements arising from appraisal are few and far between. However, they do arise and have to be prepared for.

In an appraisal system which is linked in some way to pay, bonus or grading, where people feel that there is a lot riding on the outcome, some form of appeals procedure for people who disagree with the rating they have been given is essential. This need not be elaborate – in most organisations it is based on the existing grievance procedure.

Disagreement is most likely to occur between an appraiser and appraisee about a rating, a grading given, or about how well an objective has been achieved. If, after discussion, they are unable to resolve it between themselves the appraisee must have the right of appeal to higher authority. At each stage it is to be hoped that agreement can be reached but if not, the appeal should be moved up to the next stage. The highest level for an appeal in many organisations would be an appeals panel, convened for the purpose of arbitrating on appeals arising from appraisals. This panel would usually consist of senior managers, personnel specialists and employee representatives.

A typical procedure would consist of the following process:
- a meeting with the manager's manager;
- a meeting with the divisional, or business unit head;
- a meeting with a senior personnel manager;
- an appeal to a specially convened appeals panel.

At all stages, the emphasis should be on conciliation not confrontation. It is important to remember that the process from which the disagreement arose is about appraisal and is not a disciplinary situation. If employees get the feeling that appeals are not treated seriously, it can cast doubt across the whole of the appraisal system. Although every effort must be made to make appraisal as objective as possible, it has to be acknowledged that even the very best are to some extent subjective.

An organisation which has built a climate of openness and trust with employees will find that disagreements arising from appraisals are the exception rather than the rule. A company of some 2,000 employees introduced an appraisal system for the first time, covering white and blue collar employees. This system was directly linked to a process of performance related pay. After the first round of appraisals, only three employees felt the need to take their disagreements to the appeals panel. This company committed a lot of time, effort and resources to communications and training and gained the benefit from this.

Chapter 6

APPRAISAL IN ACTION

An important element in any appraisal system is the form that is used. The form gives meaning to the overall objectives of the system, it provides a structure for the appraisal interview and it demonstrates to the appraisee what the organisation is interested in. This latter point is most important in terms of measuring performance. If the form contains performance rating categories, the message received by employees is likely to be that these are the categories that the organisation considers to be most important.

Great care is therefore required in designing the form to be used because the messages it conveys go beyond it just being a form which is used for appraisal.

Four examples of different types of appraisal form follow, with a brief explanation and comment on each one. Four quite different approaches have been selected in order to give readers an insight into the range of approaches which are used. No attempt has been made to evaluate the forms in comparison with each other – this could only be done if we were party to the objectives which led to the design of each form.

EXAMPLE 1

A simple, straightforward form, easy to complete, aimed at assessing people in management grades, although there is no apparent reason why this form should not be used with other grades of staff.

Comments

- There appears to be no opportunity for self-appraisal other than during the appraisal interview, and one must wonder how easy it would be for the appraisee to comment at this stage if they have not been encouraged to prepare for the interview.

- Under section 2 the appraiser is asked to rate the performance of the job holder but there is no indication of how to assess performance or what high or low performance would look like. It is possible that this type of information may have been conveyed to the appraiser in a separate document; if not, the fear must be that different appraisers would assess performance in different ways.

- The job holder is asked to sign the form half way through the interview – does this imply that the job holder does not see the remainder of the form when it has been completed? Questions 4, 5 and 6 lend themselves ideally to the involvement of the job holder – in fact, it is difficult to imagine them being completed without this involvement.

EXAMPLE 1

PERFORMANCE APPRAISAL   **MANAGERIAL GRADES**

1.   APPRAISEE'S NAME: APPRAISAL DATE:

      JOB TITLE: DEPARTMENT:

      APPRAISER'S NAME:

      APPRAISER'S JOB TITLE:

---

2.   WRITE A BRIEF SUMMARY OF THE JOB HOLDER'S PERFORMANCE AS ASSESSED
      DURING THE PERIOD UNDER REVIEW. NOTE IN PARTICULAR ANY HIGH/LOW
      POINTS IN PERFORMANCE.

---

3.   ANY OTHER COMMENTS (including those of the Job Holder)

Signature of Job Holder .... Signature of Appraiser ....

4. What are the Job Holder's major strong points?

5. In what areas could the Job Holder's performance be improved?

6. Note any education, training or other action you may wish to recommend which will benefit the appraisee and the Company. Please give some idea of priority or degree of urgency.

EXAMPLE 2

This is an interesting form and is easy to complete. However, some of the information required is rather more difficult to assess and be objective about.

Comments

- Self-assessment is used in this example although it is unclear what influence this has on the rest of the appraisal interview. It seems to be restricted to a separate part of the appraisal and although it may influence the interview it does not seem to to be designed to run through the process.

- The first part of the appraiser's assessment is concerned with career potential and asks for some very specific assessments. It is unusual for this element to appear before the assessment of performance and may be taken to indicate that the overriding purpose of the appraisal is to assess potential for promotion.

- For an appraiser to be asked about a likely successor for someone who might be promoted is also unusual – in many cases the appraiser would not have a sufficient knowl-edge of the full range of likely candidates to be able to make this judgement.

- Job performance is assessed and some examples of how the appraiser should think about performance is given, although the response to such broad questions suggests that the answers will be highly subjective.

- A minor point is that there is a danger that using numbers for two separate purposes on the form could lead to some confusion. They are used to indicate sections and to record levels of performance under the 'unsatisfactory' heading.

- It appears that the appraisee does not see the completed form as the signature is only required on the self-assessment. Does this mean that the other elements are not even discussed with the appraisee?

- Comments are made by a senior manager but who else sees them?

EXAMPLE 2

PERFORMANCE APPRAISAL REVIEW

Name:

Job title: Location:

Age: Years in present job: Years with company:

Date of appraisal review:

Name of appraiser:

Period covered:

SECTION 1   SELF-ASSESSMENT

1.   What were your agreed targets during the last period?

2.   To what degree did you achieve your targets?

3.   Highlight any other significant achievements that you have accomplished during the last period.

4.   What difficulties affecting job performance have you encountered and why?

5.   Which of your abilities are not being fully utilised in your present role?

6.   What skills or knowledge do you need to improve or acquire now or in the future?

7.   What other matters would you like to discuss?

Appraisee's signature .... Date ....

SECTION 2   APPRAISER'S ASSESSMENT

1.   Career potential

Should this person be considered for further development and/or promotion within the next three years?

If yes, please state:

– Likely next move

– When should this be?

– What further skills or abilities will need to be acquired?

If no, please state reasons for your views:

2.   Successor

Who is this person's most likely successor?

When will they be ready?

3.   Job performance in the last period

Please identify the performance rating you award by putting a circle around the appropriate letter and number below.

A   **Exceptional performance** – outstanding performance which consistently exceeds the required standards.

B   **Good performance** – generally exceeds the required standards.

C   **Acceptable performance** – meets acceptable standards most of the time but at times requires improvement and support.

D   Unsatisfactory performance – fails to meet performance standards.

   1   Conscientious and hard working.

   2   Achieves an adequate output for most activities.

   3   Needs constant direction and supervision.

Please explain the comments made above:

Any further information or comments which you feel should be taken into account:

Appraiser's signature .... Date ....

4.   Senior manager's comments

Signature .... Date ....

EXAMPLE 3

This provides a more complex approach which clearly requires some thought before completion. Not enough space is provided on the section for the rating scales and the self-appraisal and the manager's appraisal marks are too close together.

Comments

- The form requires ten rating scales to be completed which seem to be awarded equal importance, although they could be said to be of variable importance in terms of their impact and importance to a business. Perhaps there should be some way of weighting the scores for each scale.

- The appraiser and appraisee are both asked to assess performance but how this should be done and what should constitute the award of any of the performance levels is not clear. This may mean that the two parties make highly subjective judgements based on their assessment of what constitutes each particular performance level, potentially leading to disagreements.

- The appraisee participates fully in the process as far as rating of performance, objective setting and training requirements are concerned.

- It is not clear what happens after the form has been signed by the departmental manager, but it appears that these comments would not be fed back to the appraisee.

EXAMPLE 3

STAFF APPRAISAL FORM – STRICTLY CONFIDENTIAL

FOR THE PERIOD_____ GRADE_____ Start Date_____

Staff Appraisal Form For:_____ Staff No: _____

Completed By: _____ Date: _____

Consider each of the following questions and award an appraisal score in the appropriate box for each one.

Code: E = Excellent, G = Good, S = Satisfactory, F = Fair, P = Poor

1.   QUALITY OF WORK

Does the quality of work meet the standard required?

Self appraisal	E ❑	G ❑	S ❑	F ❑	P ❑
Manager's appraisal	E ❑	G ❑	S ❑	F ❑	P ❑

Remarks: _____

2.   QUANTITY OF WORK

Does the quantity of work meet the standard required?

Self appraisal	E ❑	G ❑	S ❑	F ❑	P ❑
Manager's appraisal	E ❑	G ❑	S ❑	F ❑	P ❑

Remarks: _____

3.   JOB KNOWLEDGE

Are the necessary skills and knowledge consistently displayed and applied in doing the job?

Self appraisal	E ❑	G ❑	S ❑	F ❑	P ❑
Manager's appraisal	E ❑	G ❑	S ❑	F ❑	P ❑

Remarks: _____

4.   INITIATIVE/INDEPENDENCE

Does the appraisee consistently apply initiative and ability to work effectively while unsupervised?

Self appraisal	E ❑	G ❑	S ❑	F ❑	P ❑
Manager's appraisal	E ❑	G ❑	S ❑	F ❑	P ❑

Remarks: _____

5. RELATIONSHIPS WITH OTHERS

Does the appraisee demonstrate an ability to work effectively with other people, managers, peers and subordinates?

Self appraisal   E ❑   G ❑   S ❑   F ❑   P ❑
Manager's appraisal   E ❑   G ❑   S ❑   F ❑   P ❑

Remarks: _____

6. LOYALTY AND COMMITMENT

Does the appraisee demonstrate loyalty to the company and commitment to work?

Self appraisal   E ❑   G ❑   S ❑   F ❑   P ❑
Manager's appraisal   E ❑   G ❑   S ❑   F ❑   P ❑

Remarks: _____

7. TIMEKEEPING AND PUNCTUALITY

Does the appraisee consistently demonstrate punctuality and good timekeeping?

Self appraisal   E ❑   G ❑   S ❑   F ❑   P ❑
Manager's appraisal   E ❑   G ❑   S ❑   F ❑   P ❑

Remarks: _____

8. LEADERSHIP

Does the appraisee demonstrate the ability to lead a team effectively?

Self appraisal   E ❑   G ❑   S ❑   F ❑   P ❑
Manager's appraisal   E ❑   G ❑   S ❑   F ❑   P ❑

Remarks: _____

9. PLANNING AND COORDINATION

Does the appraisee plan and coordinate tasks effectively and efficiently?

Self appraisal   E ❑   G ❑   S ❑   F ❑   P ❑
Manager's appraisal   E ❑   G ❑   S ❑   F ❑   P ❑

Remarks: _____

10. TRAINING AND DEVELOPMENT

Does the appraisee demonstrate a desire to develop and adapt for possible future assignments?

Self appraisal   E ❑   G ❑   S ❑   F ❑   P ❑
Manager's appraisal   E ❑   G ❑   S ❑   F ❑   P ❑

Remarks: _____

OBJECTIVES FOR COMING YEAR

_____
_____
_____
_____
_____
_____
_____
_____
_____

TRAINING REQUIREMENTS IN COMING YEAR

_____
_____
_____
_____
_____
_____
_____
_____
_____

SIGNED BY APPRAISER_____   SIGNED BY APPRAISEE_____

DATE _____   DATE _____

COMMENTS BY DEPARTMENTAL MANAGER / FURTHER ACTIONS REQUIRED

_____
_____
_____
_____
_____
_____

SIGNED / APPROVED BY _____   DATE_____

PERSONNEL DEPARTMENT RECORDS

EXAMPLE 4

This is by far the longest form we have looked at, requiring fairly detailed consideration before completion. The length of the form is influenced by the generous allocation of space to the various sections. This aids clarity but the length may put some people off.

Comments

- Self-appraisal is an important element of the form. It is clear what is being asked for and the Lowest and Highest score indicators help in identifying how to assess performance on each rating scale.

- As well as the indicators the form asks for the rating to be assessed on a numerical scale rather than as in example number 3, which uses words to describe the performance. Some people believe that the use of numbers leads to a more objective score being awarded. This view is based on the idea that it is easier and more acceptable for people to score themselves 2 or 3, rather than fair or poor.

- There are fourteen rating scales, which seems rather a lot, and although some may be marked 'not applicable', it is difficult to see which ones may not apply to all, other than the final one which refers to managing people. The scales do, however, all seem to relate to important business issues which an organisation should expect people to perform in.

- Section B asks for an overall assessment to be made by the appraiser which may provide some useful additional information.

- Section C asks for the appraisee to comment on their level of job satisfaction, which is an interesting and unusual addition and may provide information for a discussion during the appraisal interview.

- Overall the approach is very appraisee centred. The career and development section encourages the appraisee to take more ownership than is often the case and there is a provision for final comments from the appraisee.

- A copy of the form is to be given to the appraisee at the end of the process indicating that they will see the comments made by the senior manager.

EXAMPLE 4

Performance Appraisal

Name _____ Job title _____

Division _____ In current position since _____

How long
Date joined _____ worked for interviewer _____

Date of last appraisal _____

Interviewer's name _____ Interviewer's position _____

Date of interview _____ Period under review _____ to _____

A. Performance rating

Appraisal Score	Self appraisal Score	Lowest score indicator	1 2 3 4 5 6	Highest score indicator

Mark N/A if not applicable

1 Relationships with internal and external customers

☐ ☐

Has been insensitive and tactless, tended to say or do the wrong thing at the wrong time

Has been sensitive and tactful, consistently used the appropriate behaviour to deal with all levels of staff and customers

2 Knowledge and skills

☐ ☐

Has had difficulty in acquiring and applying appropriate knowledge and skills and generally required assistance to resolve problems

Consistently acquired and applied appropriate knowledge to the effective solution of customer/company needs and problems with little or no assistance

3 Attitude and commitment

☐ ☐

Has shown a negative attitude, been unconcerned about personal standards, lacked commitment to tasks and/or the company

Has consistently displayed a positive attitude and high personal standards. Has made a positive contribution to all tasks and demonstrates a high level of commitment to the company

4 Decision making

☐ ☐

Has avoided making decisions or made poor decisions

Has been an outstanding decision maker, always basing decisions on the soundest evidence

5 Relationships with colleagues

☐ ☐

Has chosen to work alone and generally distanced from colleagues; has been prone to generate strain or conflict in relationships

Has fitted readily into the team and demonstrated a marked facility for developing effective relationships

Appraisal Score	Self appraisal Score	Lowest score indicator	1 2 3 4 5 6	Highest score indicator
6 Personal impact ☐	☐	Has failed to persuade others to change minds; colleagues and customers have usually failed to take note of opinion		Has usually persuaded colleagues and customers to go along with their views
7 Conceptual ability ☐	☐	Has used only a routine, unoriginal approach to situations and opportunities		Has consistently delivered original and innovative approaches to situations and challenges
8 Setting and meeting priorities ☐	☐	Has failed to allocate time effectively with result that work is disorganised and time wasted		Has consistently demonstrated an ability accurately to establish priorities, to manage time effectively and to overcome obstacles
9 Effectiveness within systems ☐	☐	Has created needless work for others, showing lack of regard for necessary administrative systems		Has achieved harmony by achieving goals without harming appropriate administrative systems
10 Accuracy and quality ☐	☐	Has not completed work allocated to the level of accuracy and quality required		Consistently completed all work allocated to accuracy and quality required
11 Task completion ☐	☐	Has not completed tasks, assignments within an acceptable timescale		Has consistently completed tasks and assignments well within expected timescales

Appraisal Score	Self appraisal Score	Lowest score indicator	1 2 3 4 5 6	Highest score indicator

12 Commercial and entrepreneurial flair

☐   ☐

Has failed to show any evidence of identifying business opportunities

Has identified and converted business opportunities with new and existing customers and suppliers

13 Customer credibility

☐   ☐

Has usually failed to understand and meet customer requirements

Has usually understood and exceeded customer requirements. Has earned the customer's trust and respect

14 Managing subordinates

☐   ☐

Has not controlled, communicated, delegated or trained effectively

Has exercised control, communicated and trained effectively and delegated appropriately

Total scores

☐   ☐

Number of questions completed

☐

Average scores

☐   ☐

B. Overall performance assessment

Written comments to explain or clarify scores given above. Also comment on any additional information not covered above

C. Job satisfaction

How do you rate your current level of job satisfaction, on a scale of 1-6?

Very   1   2   3   4   5   6   Very
unhappy   happy

D. Career development/training requirements

1   Describe how you would like to see your career develop within the company.

2   Identify and describe any training (internal and external) you feel would help you in your job. This could be achieved by working in other parts of the business, more help on the job and so on.

E. Objectives for the next six month period

At least four objectives should be set. Information gained in the performance rating may be used as a basis.

Interviewer's comments

Signed   Dated

Interviewee's comments

I have read the above and wish to add the following comments (if any)

Signed   Dated

Comments by interviewer's manager

Signed   Dated

NB   *A copy of this form should be given to the interviewee, the original to be kept in the interviewee's personnel file.*

CONCLUSIONS

The four examples given are very different and all have their merits; all will have been designed to meet the specific objectives of the organisation they are used by. It is important to decide what you want to get from your appraisal system and then design a form which will deliver this.

Chapter 7

DEFINING PERFORMANCE MEASURES AND SETTING OBJECTIVES

MEASURING PERFORMANCE

Measuring performance in a way which is acceptable to the performer and to the requirements of an appraisal is clearly not as easy as the old adage *'Anything which can be managed can be measured'* maintains. Try defining service measures which can be applied to service in shops, retail financial services or any of the many areas of working life where a service provider interacts directly with the customer. It is easy enough to define measures to cover the sales or the number of customers handled, but not so easy to measure the level of service. Many organisations now employ companies to act as 'mystery shoppers', to give them some objectivity in their measures. When first introduced, this type of approach was viewed with suspicion, but they are now generally accepted as making an important contribution to a more objective approach to measurement. Measuring performance, however, is the key to effective appraisal, so even if it is difficult, organisations have to persevere with the task of defining appropriate measures.

In developing measures one of the most important things we have to do is to make sure that the measures we agree are meaningful and make a really important contribution to the success of the job. Because of the difficulty of agreeing appropriate measures, too many people accept second best and employ measures and objectives which are not critical to the job. For a measure or objective to be useful it has to be relevant and critical to the successful outcome of the job.

A starting point in defining job related measures is to establish standards of performance. A standard of performance states what constitutes acceptable performance in a particular task or in working towards a specific objective. This means that the job holder has to be informed about some basic information about the requirements of the job. If an individual does not know what constitutes the acceptable standard to which the job must be done it is unreasonable to criticise them for not achieving this.

So the first step in defining measures for job performance is to establish standards of performance for each job.

Key results areas

Every job consists of a range of tasks and it is not unusual for some of these tasks to be more important than others. This is certainly true of the majority of management jobs and also for many professional workers. Following the suggestion above, that each task should have clearly defined standards of performance, how do we move from this to ensuring the job holder concentrates sufficient effort to getting right those things which are really critical to the success of the job?

One way of doing this is to develop, for each job, a set of **key result areas**; these can be described as those elements of the job which are critical to the successful outcome of the job. Key result areas are defined by understanding the job and then being able to focus on those areas which are considered to be the most important. Many would argue that if you understand the key result areas and measure them effectively, it is not necessary to be too concerned about those other aspects of the job. This may well be true for the majority of management jobs where it is essential to concentrate on doing those things which make a real difference, and placing a focus on performance measures and objectives greatly helps this process.

The process for achieving this can be described as follows:

- Conduct a detailed analysis of each job so that there is a real understanding about what constitutes the tasks and the outcomes.

- Identify the principal accountabilities and principal tasks.

- Define standards of performance for each task.

- Concentrate on the critical outcomes and agree with the job holder what the key result areas are.

- Define performance measures for the key result areas and agree these with the job holder.

If all of this is done successfully, each job will have a set of key performance measures against which the performance of the job holder can be compared at the end of the agreed period.

SETTING OBJECTIVES

The starting point has to be to understand just what is meant by an objective.

An objective is a statement of a result to be achieved. If it is to be measurable, it is necessary for the objective to include a specified time for completion and other yardsticks which allow the individual and the manager to know when it has been achieved.

Objectives fall into five broad categories. Every job has its routine aspects but also scope for problem solving and innovation; most jobs also involve responding to objectives which are cascaded throughout the organisation. In addition, individuals will want to consider objectives which relate to development needs.

Using this approach we can look to set objectives in the following broad areas of job responsibility:

- routine job responsibilities;

- problem solving;

- innovation;
- cascaded objectives;
- personal development.

It helps to think about these broad areas when contemplating which objectives to set. Some examples of typical objectives might be:

- *Personal development* – to successfully complete the National Vocational Qualification in retail service by the end of December.

- *Routine* – to complete all departmental appraisal interviews by the end of November.

- *Problem solving* – to review and evaluate the existing procedures for invoice payments and make recommendations for a procedure designed to increase the level of payments received within 30 days from the present level of 45% to a level of 80%. The recommendations to be ready for approval by October 31 and implementation immediately thereafter.

These are examples and each person who is responsible for setting objectives should give serious thought to what they want to achieve and set their objectives accordingly.

A useful way of thinking about objectives is to keep in mind that objectives are concerned with outputs, the results of activity. Difficulty appears to be caused by confusing outputs with inputs or activities. The activity is, of course, important but the objective has to be concerned with identifying and describing the output of the activity, not the activity itself.

Far too often objectives are set which do not enable output to be measured, and if you are unable to identify, describe and measure the output you have probably set an activity, not an objective.

The three examples shown above each describe what is to be achieved and by when, so at the due date for each, the interested parties will easily be able to identify if they have achieved the objective or not.

Other useful ways of looking at objectives are:

Objectives must be MARC:

- *Measurable* – how will the individual know when the objective has been achieved?
- *Achievable* – must be within the capacity of the individual to achieve.
- *Relevant* – must be relevant to the job responsibilities of the individual.
- *Controllable* – must be within the control of the individual.

Objectives must be SMART:

- *Specific* – must relate to clearly identifiable elements of a job.
- *Measurable* – see above.

- *Attainable* – see achievable above.

- *Realistic* – must be seen to be useful to achieve.

- *Time phased* – must state a time for when they should have been achieved.

In addition to the above, effective objectives should be challenging – if they fail to stretch they will not motivate the individual to achieve them.

A checklist for effective objectives

You can test the effectiveness of your objective setting by asking each of the following questions about each one. If the answer is yes to all of the questions your objectives live up to the requirements.

- Does the objective relate to the needs of the organisation?

- Does the objective relate to the job responsibilities of the individual?

- Is it challenging but also realistic and achievable?

- Is it stated in a positive way? Objectives should seek to positively influence the behaviour of the individual.

- Is it acceptable to both you as the person setting the objective and to the individual who will be expected to achieve it?

- Does it encourage the achievement of personal aims, growth, knowledge or responsibility?

- Are clear dates for achievement included?

- Does it describe the outputs required?

- Does it state clear and measurable targets?

Objectives work best if they are agreed rather than imposed and during appraisal it will always be useful to encourage appraisees to think about objectives for themselves. They can then be discussed at the appraisal meeting and agreed. This way the objectives are more likely to be acceptable to both parties and therefore more likely to be achieved.

Chapter 8

THE LINKS BETWEEN OTHER MANAGEMENT PROCESSES AND PERFORMANCE APPRAISAL

LOOKING AT THE LINKS

As well as being designed to focus the attention of individuals and their managers on improving performance, appraisal has a role to play in delivering improvements in many other areas of the organisation. Appraisal is a process which enables an organisation to collect large amounts of information which can be used to improve the way it operates in related areas of people management. These include:

- identification of potential;

- human resource planning;

- the internal job market;

- recruitment;

- training and development;

- the identification of training needs.

While none of these are or should be the primary driving force for the development of a system of appraisal, they are all processes which are important in the management of an organisation, to which appraisal can influence and provide a useful contribution.

IDENTIFICATION OF POTENTIAL

Most appraisal systems include some element of the identification of potential and it is easy to see that appraisal lends itself, in many ways ideally, to doing this. There are, however, dangers. While it is appropriate for a manager to assess and comment on the immediate past and current performance of the people who report to them, it is an entirely different matter for the manager to be expected to predict the likely success of the individual in the future.

Many managers find this a difficult part of the process and are only too aware of the expectations of the individuals they are assessing. The information training managers receive in assessing potential is frequently inadequate and gets lost in all of the other elements of the appraisal, which are deemed to be more important to cover on what is usually too short a training programme.

So let us have a look at what the identification of potential is all about. Essentially what the organisation wants is to get some idea of the promotability of its employees. This can and often does extend to asking the manager to assess the long-term potential of individuals to move into senior management positions, way above the the current level of the appraiser. Basic common sense suggests that to be able to do this successfully would require the appraiser to have much more information than is generally available about the nature of the senior management job.

From the point of view of the organisation, one can see why this type of information may be seen to be useful. It would be clearly useful to know if, out there, in various parts of the organisation there were lots of people with the potential to succeed, pushing for promotion to senior management levels. The organisation could then decide to provide further development and training opportunities for these people to equip them to progress or, in a worst case scenario, get rid of some of them if it perceived itself to be over supplied.

The key question, however, is, *'how effective and useful are these long-term predictions?'* When made by people untrained in techniques of prediction and equipped only with information gleaned from the past performance of the person they are appraising, can they be expected to make a useful contribution? Any evidence we have available to us suggests that this type of long-term prediction is not very useful. It should be remembered that managers who are asked to make this type of prediction are asked to do so on the basis of inadequate information about the nature of senior management jobs and about what may be expected of the individual in the future. How can they know what the demands of a senior job may be like in, say, five years time? They are asked to base the prediction on information which is fundamentally flawed in its ability to predict. Past performance in one job is not a good predictor of performance in other unrelated jobs. When a prediction is expected for events which may be some years away and for roles which the appraiser probably does not understand, the likelihood of the prediction being valid is negligible.

The other area where the appraiser is frequently asked to make predictions is that of suitability for the next job. We saw in Chapter 6, in Example 2 of the appraisal forms we reviewed, a specific question about the development or promotion of the appraisee within the next three years. On the face of it, this appears to be a much more reasonable expectation. Any manager should be able to make some assessment of the people who report to them with a view to how they are likely to perform in a new job. Where that new job is closely related to the current one, past performance may well be a good predictor. Frequently, however, predictions have to be made about how people will perform in completely different jobs.

The situation which causes the most difficulty is where good performance in a technical role is the basis on which future management or supervisory responsibility is made. Unfortunately, promotion into a role which involves managing people based solely on past performance is not a reliable predictor. In fact it is generally recognised that it is likely to be a poor predictor of future performance and may lead to individuals being promoted to the level of their incompetence.

None of this is intended to imply that the appraisal process should never be used to assess an individual's capability for promotion. Or, even more importantly, should not be used to discuss the appraisee's aspirations, development needs and plans. A discussion about what an appraisee aspires to is an essential part of appraisal. Equally it is not unreasonable for the organisation to expect the appraiser to offer some judgements about the potential of the person being appraised.

What is required is a certain amount of caution about what happens with the judgements once they have been made. If the judgement made at appraisal fits with other evidence which may be available from assessment centres, work in project groups, personal commitment evidenced by personal development activities, peer and team assessment, then the judgement is likely to be much more reliable.

HUMAN RESOURCE PLANNING

Human resource planning is the process by which an organisation plans its future needs in relation to matching people to jobs and ensuring that there are sufficient numbers of people with the right skills and experience to meet future requirements. Future human resource requirements must be considered in relation to:

- changes in organisation needs, as far as these can be predicted;

- the corporate plan;

- organisational development issues;

- the most appropriate age profile;

- training and development requirements.

A key element in capturing much of the information required for this planning process is the appraisal system. Appraisal provides at least once each year a wealth of practical information concerning the age, location, experience and performance of all employees. In addition it provides insights into some of the more intangible issues such as aspirations, development and training needs.

It is not difficult to see how the appraisal system, if it is effective, can help make sure that all of this information is brought together, analysed and used to help the organisation to improve its understanding of the current workforce and therefore the way it plans its human resource needs for the future.

THE INTERNAL JOBS MARKET

Most organisations actively encourage employees to move around within the company to further their career, both in seeking promotion or in attempting to broaden and deepen their experience. The cost of recruitment is a driving force in the importance some organisations place on the internal jobs market. Equally important for many organisations is the motivational benefits to be gained when people successfully transfer from one part of the organisation to another, benefits not only to the individual, but also to the many other people who see such movements as an inspiration and role model for themselves. So the internal job market plays an important role in retaining valuable experience and in motivating employees in many organisations.

An active internal jobs market is likely to:

- help retain good people;

- provide motivation for a wide range of people wanting to shape a career;

- stimulate loyalty to the organisation;

- make the process of human resource planning easier;

- act as a stimulus for training and development.

Of course there are also disadvantages:

- the danger of fitting jobs to existing skills rather than going outside to find people with the right skills;

- not bringing in enough new blood;

- the danger of creating an escalator view of career progression with less emphasis on performance than on time served.

Given the changes which have taken place in recent years with less emphasis being placed on long-term careers with one organisation, the idea of the internal jobs market may well have less significance in the future.

The link between the internal jobs market and appraisal is essentially one which relates to human resource planning. Appraisal can provide the planners with a lot of useful information about the aspirations, intentions and plans of people which can be incorporated into the human resource plan.

RECRUITMENT

Recruitment is a major area of cost for many organisations and few, if any, can afford the luxury of getting it wrong too often. Any internal mechanism which can contribute to more effective recruitment is therefore to be welcomed. Appraisal can do this in a number of ways: centrally for the organisation as a whole, and locally where individual managers are responsible for recruiting staff.

Centrally, the main impact can be seen in terms of the planning process. In much the same way as the information gleaned from appraisal can influence the internal jobs market, so it can also contribute to the recruitment plan. As stated above, an appraisal system provides a lot of information and if this is used effectively, in time it can help to identify potential skill shortages which can be met by training rather than recruitment.

Any information which adds clarity to the human resource plan can be a valuable aid to helping the organisation manage its human resource costs.

Locally, many managers have a responsibility for recruiting staff and the relationship between recruitment and appraisal can be important. This can be seen in the way it helps managers to deepen their understanding of the skills required in various jobs, how people actually do their job and the application of the skills required. All of this information is invaluable when a manager has to draw up a new job description and personnel specification when the need for a new recruit has been identified.

TRAINING AND DEVELOPMENT

Most people recognise the very clear relationship between the appraisal process and the training and development provision of the organisation. There are two ways this can be seen:

- the central identification of training needs for the organisation;

- the opportunity provided to individuals to focus on and discuss their training and development needs.

Identification of training needs

It is frequently necessary to look at training needs across the organisation as a whole, where, for example, the organisation is seeking to meet certain priorities within a specified time or where a new product or process is being introduced. At such times, the training department needs to have a clear picture of the numbers and locations of those requiring training and the current skill levels of those involved.

The appraisal can provide this information swiftly and conveniently. Most organisations also need to monitor the ongoing training of staff in various standard skills which are important to maintain at defined levels. The appraisal provides an opportunity to review this position at least once each year. It enables the detail of the training plan for the following year to be prepared and for judgements to be made about demand for specific requirements as well as identifying requests for new programmes to be developed.

It is now popular for training to be more demand driven than previously. This means that instead of the training department issuing a list of programmes which will be run during the next period, training prepares its plans in response to what managers identify as the key needs for training. This is a more healthy approach as it makes training provision responsive to the needs of the line management, but without an appraisal system as a means of gathering the data it would be difficult to deliver.

Identifying key competencies which employees need to achieve at various stages in their career is a way in which organisations are managing employee development. Competencies have the benefit of bringing together technical and professional skills with behavioural and management skills. They are frequently set out in a format which allows people at various levels in the organisation to identify the competencies they require in relation to their current job. In many cases, they also describe the competencies which would be required in a job which the individual may aspire to.

During an appraisal meeting the competencies can be used to help an individual appraisee to focus on the skill and knowledge they need to acquire to become fully competent in their current role as well as planning for the future. An appraisal system enables the information to be captured and used centrally to build a greater understanding about the competence base of the organisation as a whole, as well as providing focus on the needs of the individual.

The development of individuals

For all the benefits and importance of the points made above about the identification of training needs, one of the most important outcomes of appraisal should be that it encourages each individual to focus on their own development. The key questions which can be posed at appraisal are:

- What do you want to achieve in terms of your career?

- In the short and the long-term?

- What skills, knowledge, competencies will you need to develop to enable you to achieve this, in the short and the long-term?

- Where are you starting from, what skills, knowledge, competence do you have now?

- How do these contribute to your short and long-term aspirations?

- Can you identify any gaps?

- What plans do you need to make to bridge the gaps?

- How will you do it?

- When will you start?

- What help and support can I give?

The purpose of this type of question is threefold: they help the appraisee to focus on what they actually want to achieve; they encourage the appraisee to identify gaps between current knowledge, skill and competence, and desired knowledge, skill and competence; they place ownership for development firmly in the hands of the individual.

For too long, too many organisations and managers encouraged people to believe that *the organisation* would look after the development needs of all. This was never true and should never have been the impression that was created. Many people, however, believed it and handed over responsibility for their development to others, who were believed to know best. This view has now largely vanished and people are expected to manage their own careers and development.

They do, however, need help – someone to bounce ideas off, someone who may have a better understanding of what is available, someone who may have access to different, wider networks. Appraisal can provide an opportunity to explore all of this. This is not to suggest that the appraiser will necessarily be all of these 'someones', but the appraiser may well be able to open up a contact with the right people.

Appraisal should be seen as a key element in personal development planning and for this reason many organisations have separated the development part of appraisal from the performance assessment part. This is understandable, but not essential. However, the difficulties it overcomes are as follows:

- The emphasis on performance can divert the attention of both the appraiser and appraisee from development, both in preparation and during the meeting.

- The time required to cover both elements at the same meeting frequently leads to the development element of the appraisal not getting the attention it requires.

Appraisal, then, plays an important role in the whole area of training and development. The contribution it can make to ensuring the relevance of training and development activities at an organisational and at a personal level are hard to overstate.

Chapter 9

THE PERFORMANCE REVIEW INTERVIEW

INTRODUCTION

A key element in any appraisal is the meeting which takes place between the appraiser and the appraisee. In many ways the success or failure of the whole process rests on how well this interview is conducted. In Chapter 1 a comment was made that any system is only as good as the people who are responsible for operating it. It is at this stage, where the interview takes place, that control shifts from the designers of the process into the hands of the implementers. The success or failure of the process as seen by the appraisee now rests on how well this interview is handled.

If the interview does not work well, meeting the needs and expectations of both parties, the whole process is likely to fall into disrepute. This is unfortunately what happens in many organisations. The manager responsible for doing the appraisal is ill prepared and ill equipped to do a good job. Likewise the person being appraised has confused expectations and because of this frequently fails to think through what they want to get from the meeting. The better prepared both parties are, the more effective the meeting will be.

The way organisations can influence the appraiser and appraisee to think about and plan for the performance review meeting has been covered in Chapter 5, where a detailed plan for communications was outlined. Assuming that this approach or something similar has taken place, we can be sure that at least the appraisers and appraisees know enough about the purpose and the process to make it work. What we now have to do is to consider how they take this on and make the process a success.

PREPARING FOR THE APPRAISAL INTERVIEW

We want to consider both long-term and short-term preparation for both the appraiser and the appraisee.

Long-term preparation – appraisee

Long-term preparation for the appraisee is concerned with the way each individual works during the year leading up to the review meeting. How far have they achieved the objectives which were set at the previous appraisal? Have they been working towards improving their performance along the lines agreed at the last meeting? What about those things which were agreed about personal development? Have the necessary actions been taken to continue with the process of growth and development?

The achievement of aspirations by any individual is to a very large extent in their own hands. If they fail to grasp opportunities for training and development, if they fail to pursue studies which they agreed to undertake, then what they aspire to will not be achieved. Of course, the organisation has a responsibility to provide opportunities for development, the responsibility to help individuals work towards further growth in knowledge and skill. Fundamentally, however, the day has long gone when an individual joined an organisation and handed over to the organisation the responsibility for the long-term development of their career. The individual today must take on the responsibility for their own career development and an appraisal meeting should be seen as a milestone on the way.

More specific preparation for the appraisee will be in the way they seek to persuade their manager to recognise the achievements they make with objectives and improvements in performance.

Long-term preparation – appraiser

For the appraiser the long-term preparation has to be more considered and detailed. As in the case of the appraisee, the preparation is essentially concerned with objectives achieved and performance improved. These two factors have to be noted, recorded and become the subject of feedback to the individual concerned.

Long-term preparation is essentially the day-to-day management of people; it should cover an awareness of and concern for the achievement of objectives and improvements in performance. Many managers find it useful to make an occasional note about performance as the year progresses, as it is always difficult to recall key events when the appraisal meeting comes around. Without some means of recording the events of the year the appraisal meeting can deteriorate into a vague and meaningless discussion without a clear agenda and structure.

For many, a way in which the annual meeting can be made much more meaningful is to hold two or three other, shorter meetings to review progress during the year. If this is done on a regular basis the annual meeting becomes a more natural continuation of a constant review of performance. It loses any fears it may hold, and the people concerned will be more open as it will be seen as a continuous process rather than a one-off irregular event.

An agenda for an interim appraisal meeting is given below.

1. Identify and agree examples of positive performance improvements observed during the last period.

2. Identify and discuss any examples of negative performance observed during the last period. Discuss and agree any actions which the appraisee can take to eliminate these during the next period.

3. Review the objectives which were agreed at the last meeting.

   • Have these been achieved?

- Are there any factors external to the appraisee limiting the achievement of objectives?

- Are the objectives still relevant?

- Do they need to be amended in the light of any changes in the circumstances of the job?

- Identify, agree and record any significant changes to existing objectives, set new objectives if appropriate.

4. Review plans for personal development agreed at the last meeting.

- Have these been achieved?

- Have any plans for training or coaching on the job to improve performance been implemented?

- Is now the appropriate time to agree any changes or additions to the personal development plan?

5. Summary of actions agreed.

In some instances it may be useful to give the appraisee a copy of the note of this discussion to remind them of the actions agreed. It will always be important for the manager to keep a note as it will act as part of the agenda for the next review meeting and for the main appraisal.

Many managers find it useful to hold two interim meetings each year, and some even hold three in addition to the main appraisal.

Such meetings, if held regularly, do not need to be too time consuming. In isolation and out of context of the specific situation, it is always very difficult to propose a suggested amount of time which needs to be devoted to appraisal meetings. Equally difficult is to suggest a time commitment for interim meetings. However, if such meetings are held every three or four months they should not need to take longer than fifteen or twenty minutes each time, while the main meeting could take on average forty-five to sixty minutes if the appraisal is to cover the main elements as outlined in Chapter 4.

When put like this, it is not unreasonable to expect that a manager should spend something like two hours each year with each of their people discussing performance, objectives and development. Many managers would claim that they spend a lot more than this in any case. Unfortunately, this is often largely unstructured and what the appraisal and the interim reviews try to do is to put some structure on the meetings.

SHORT-TERM PREPARATION

In discussing short-term preparation the comments will be limited to preparation for the main appraisal which in the majority of organisations will take place once every year. Where the process allows for two meetings, one to cover the review of performance and one to cover development, the preparation for both should follow the guidelines suggested.

Appraisal works best if both parties prepare for it. Too often the role of the appraisee does not receive enough attention and the idea of the appraisee preparing for appraisal is not considered seriously. Nothing could be further from the truth – it is just as important for the appraisee to prepare as for the appraiser.

Short-term preparation is intended to cover the preparation which both parties need to do in the period immediately before the appraisal meeting.

Short-term preparation – appraisee

The preparation the appraisee needs to do should follow the structure of the appraisal meeting which is usually based around the layout of the appraisal form. Examples of typical forms were shown in Chapter 6.

The appraisee needs to be honest in their preparation, especially in reviewing their performance and achievement of objectives. In organisations which include in the process an element of self-appraisal this will help to drive the preparation and to concentrate the emphasis of the preparation.

A useful plan for an appraisee to follow in preparing for appraisal could be as follows:

1. Take an honest look at how you have performed during the last period asking yourself:

   - What have been your best achievements?

   - What have you failed to do which you should have done?

   - What actions could you take to improve performance in specific areas of your work?

   - If possible, and if you feel comfortable doing it, ask colleagues to give you some feedback on how they see your performance. If you do this you need to remember that you are not looking for someone to tell you how good you are – you want an honest assessment of how they see you.

   - What help would you need in order to achieve this?

2. Review the objectives you agreed at your last appraisal meeting.

   - Have these been achieved?

   - If not, why not? What prevented the achievement. Were there any factors outside your control?

   - Are any outstanding objectives still relevant?

   - Do they need to be changed in any way?

3. What objectives would you set for yourself for the next period?

   - You should think these through in as much detail as possible. In doing this you need to follow the guidelines for effective objectives in exactly the same way as your manager would be expected to do. These are set out in Chapter 7.

4. Consider your personal and career development.

- What are your aspirations for your career? What do you want to achieve? What level would you like to reach?

- If your aspirations are to move on to a level higher than, say, the one above you, think about the steps you will need to take on the way.

- What knowledge and skills do you believe people operating at this level need to have?

- Now review your knowledge and skills. Do they match the requirements of your aspirations? Are there any gaps? What are they? Identify and note these honestly.

- What action can you take to bridge any gaps you have identified? How will you do this? Make a practical plan for action.

- What action do you need the support of your manager to take – attendance at training courses, financial support if this is available, anything else?

5. Think about what you want to have achieved by this time next year and set out a plan of action for achieving it.

If only all appraisees would approach their appraisal as well prepared as this, appraisals would be easier to conduct and much more successful in delivering the best results for the appraisee, the appraiser and the organisation.

Short-term preparation - appraiser

The appraiser needs to prepare in detail for each appraisal meeting if it is going to deliver the results required. There are a number of documents which it may be useful to look at as a starting point for this preparation:

- the appraisee's job description;
- the last appraisal;
- the objectives agreed last time;
- the appraisee's key result areas if these have been identified and agreed (see Chapter 7 for a discussion of key result areas);
- interim appraisals, if these have been conducted.

Each of these documents give the appraiser who is preparing for an appraisal a starting point from which to make some comparison between what is expected of the appraisee and what they have delivered. None of them on their own should be the only basis for the preparation but they all have some relevance.

In reviewing the appraisee's job description it is important to review it in the light of the current demands of the job. We live in a world of work which is undergoing constant and rapid change and a job description which was relevant to the job last year may now be well out of date. So we need to look at it in the light of what we expect the job holder to be doing now, not what they would have been doing at some time in the past.

The same point applies to the review of objectives. The needs of jobs move so quickly that we have to make sure that they are relevant to what we expect now, not what was expected when the objectives were set.

In looking at each of these documents the appraiser is seeking to gain and understand a point of comparison for the actual performance. As was pointed out in Chapter 2, the assessment of performance is always difficult and must, to a large extent, be subjective, therefore anything which can be used to raise the level of objectivity should be employed.

An important element which the appraiser uses in reviewing the performance of an individual is that of observation. Being aware of how people are performing by watching them work and conducting regular reviews of their work will provide the manager with a real insight into how well people are doing. This, of course, requires a close involvement by the manager with the work of the people and is not possible for every manager. Where it is possible it should be a normal part of every manager's job.

It is also important for the appraiser to review honestly those elements of the previous appraisal where they made an agreement to take some action. Did they promise to introduce the appraisee to some new skills and responsibilities? If so, did they deliver? Did they promise some off the job training and did they deliver? Questions like this have to be faced squarely and honestly; if they are dodged, the appraisee will resent being told about any shortcomings they may have while the manager's are ignored.

In most cases the manager will also need to think about the potential and promotability of the individual. What action, if any, is required in respect of this? Another reality of the modern organisation is that many are flattening their structures. This inevitably reduces the prospects of promotion for many people. A lot of people who in the past had set their sights on what may have been seen as modest progress through the organisation, may now not get that opportunity because of organisational changes. How to handle such potentially sensitive subjects during the appraisal and still have a well motivated employee at the end of the meeting requires careful thought.

If promotion is no longer an option, what other opportunities exist? Can jobs be broadened, enriched? Can more responsibility be delegated? How will this be handled during the meeting? If the meeting is not prepared, you can rest assured it will be handled badly and the appraisee will leave the meeting feeling that their concerns have received less attention than they deserved.

As with so many other things in life, preparation represents a very large part of the reason for a successful outcome. Effective preparation leads to an effective appraisal interview.

THE APPRAISAL SETTING

It is important to give adequate thought to the question of the most appropriate setting for an appraisal interview. There are some general guidelines which it will be useful to follow in thinking about where to hold the interview and the layout of the room you decide to use.

The appraisal interview should be conducted:

- in a quiet office where there will be the minimum of interruptions from the telephone or from passing visitors;

- in a neutral office, as meeting on the manager's territory can create difficulties for the appraisee – the manager will feel comfortable being in familiar surroundings while the appraisee is confronted with having to adjust to the environment.

How should the room be arranged?

- Ideally the meeting should take place with both parties sitting in comfortable chairs placed at a round table.

- If this is not possible the manager should try to reorganise the office in order to place the appraisee on a more equal footing. Two chairs placed at the end or in front of the desk is usually a good option.

- If possible, the appraiser should arrange to have coffee/tea available. This helps to create rapport and helps the appraisee to relax.

- Keep the desk or table clear of any papers which will not be required for the appraisal.

What sort of atmosphere should you aim for?

- Make sure that you allow adequate time.

- Ensure privacy.

- Promote a feeling of informality.

- Make sure you put the appraisee at ease right from the start.

- Remember that the appraisee may well be feeling ill at ease, especially if this is an unusual situation for them.

Make sure you avoid:

- a desk or table cluttered by lots of paper – it suggests that you have not prepared and are likely to be distracted by looking at the amount of work you have to do;

- sitting behind a desk, in a larger, higher, comfortable chair while the appraisee sits on a lower uncomfortable chair – an appraisal meeting is intended to get the two parties onto as equal a footing as possible.

76

CONDUCTING THE INTERVIEW

Conducting an appraisal is often described as an interview while in fact it should really be seen much more as a meeting, a somewhat more informal and equal encounter than an interview. Thinking of it as a meeting suggests that the topics to be covered will be discussed and that both parties will be involved rather than it being a one-sided process.

Although it is preferable to think of the encounter as a meeting it is still one which needs to be carefully prepared for and should have a clear structure to follow.

Structure

The structure of the meeting will generally follow the structure of the appraisal form. Most forms take a logical approach to the process and it is generally best to follow this. Flexibility and a willingness to follow the agenda of the appraisee is important, but equally it is important to cover each area required by the needs of the organisation. The structure will often follow a pattern such as the following:

- As you open the meeting, emphasise the informal nature of what you want to achieve. Stress that you want to listen and share rather than tell.

- It may be appropriate to give the appraisee some indication of the amount of time you have allowed, if you have not already done this before. This enables them to plan their agenda.

- Repeat the purpose, objectives and the process. Explain what will happen and clarify any misunderstanding about what will happen.

- Explain that it is a joint planning session and an opportunity to review performance and development plans.

- This should move on naturally into a discussion about performance during the last period and cover a review of objectives, performance in the key result areas, strengths and weaknesses, ratings if appropriate, opportunities for improvement.

- Some discussion about the organisation and the present plans for development may be appropriate.

- Career aspirations, opportunities and development needs should be covered.

- Agreement of the objectives for the next period should be reached.

- Summarise the actions agreed and what happens now.

Remember that self-appraisal is an essential technique for getting the individual talking. Ask them how they feel about the period under review, what they consider to be their strengths and weaknesses. Getting people talking encourages a feeling of involvement and commitment.

Body language

Your body language has a very important influence on the outcome of the meeting – it is essential to be aware of this and to behave accordingly. Our behaviour is everything we say and do, and includes those parts of us which are on display which other people can see and hear. It is essential to make sure that the two elements, the visual and the verbal behaviours, are kept in harmony. Too often we see a manager saying one thing and communicating through their behaviour that they actually mean something else.

An example of this which many of us have experienced is speaking to someone who is not looking at us, perhaps they are even reading or looking for a file in a filing cabinet at the same time. A typical conversation in this situation often goes, '*Carry on, I'm listening*', when you know that to be doing both things well is almost impossible. This is a clear example of the words being said and the the behaviour being displayed sending different messages.

Most people are highly sensitive to this type of contradictory behaviour and in an appraisal meeting will pick it up very quickly and very likely break off any further interest in the proceedings.

Another example of the way our body language can let us down without us realising it is the question of sincerity: the smile on the mouth, but not in the eyes; the constant repetition of good wishes in a monotone, without any attempt to support the words with behaviour which demonstrates sincerity. These and many others are clear ways to destroy confidence and the effective communication between people which appraisal is all about.

The benefit of thinking about your behaviour is that you can concentrate on using behaviour which helps you to achieve your objectives rather than behaviour which hinders. You may be in the habit of using some behaviours which give people a poor impression of you. Try to concentrate on developing some simple combinations of positive behaviours.

Some examples of behaviours designed to help a transaction and those designed to hinder a transaction follow:

Helpful behaviours

- Lean forward with hands open, arms and legs uncrossed.
- Look at the other person for approximately sixty per cent of the time.
- Smile, in a positive and encouraging way.
- Sit beside or at a 90 degree angle to the other person.
- Use the other person's name appropriately.
- Ask open questions.
- Reflect back to the other person what you believe they said.
- Use words which the other person has used.

- Demonstrate empathy.

- Give praise when it is due.

- When you agree with the other person, say so openly, and say why you agree.

- Build on the other person's ideas.

- Be non-judgemental.

- If you disagree with the other person, give the reason first, then say you disagree.

- Admit when you don't know an answer or have made a mistake.

- Make sure that your visual and verbal behaviours are in harmony.

- Show the other person the completed form and any other relevant information.

Unhelpful behaviours

- Lean away from the other person with hands clenched and arms and legs crossed tightly.

- Don't engage eye contact.

- Keep a blank expression on your face.

- Sit behind a desk or opposite the other person.

- Use the other person's name artificially so that it jars.

- Ask only closed questions.

- Don't check your understanding of what is being said.

- Stick rigidly to saying things that are routine and procedural.

- Never acknowledge the other's feelings or viewpoint.

- Only acquiesce, never explicitly agree with the other person.

- Criticise but never explain.

- Be defensive and never acknowledge any fault or inadequacy.

- Act secretively and withhold information form the other person even though it affects them.

- Display visual and verbal behaviours which are out of harmony.

- Make sure not to share ideas or papers with the other person.

Praise and criticism

An inevitable part of most appraisals is the giving of praise and criticism, and it might be thought that giving praise is easy and giving criticism is difficult. In fact, it is not as simple as this – many people find it just as difficult to give praise as to give criticism. It is, however, an issue which must be tackled as every effort should be made to ensure that the appraisal is a motivating experience.

Some guidelines for both may help.

Criticism

Criticism can be very difficult to accept – we all tend to react in a defensive way when we perceive that we are under attack. So the way the criticism is presented can greatly affect how it is received.

- Keep the exchange on an adult-to-adult basis rather than allowing it to seem like a 'ticking off'.

- Choose your words carefully.

- Try to turn a negative message into a positive action, e.g. *'How can we get your writing skills up to the same level as your telephone skills?'*

- Make sure that you treat any criticism as a process problem, not as a character defect.

- Watch the messages your body language is sending.

- Avoid using judgemental words such as 'fault', 'mistake', 'disaster'.

- Try not to express what you are saying as an opinion – stick to the facts.

Praise

We all like to receive praise and unfortunately many people at work are almost starved of any. Praise is a powerful motivator, perhaps the most powerful. It is not unusual for managers to say that they find it difficult to give praise – they feel embarrassed and don't want to seem to be patronising people. What they are actually saying is that because they don't receive enough praise themselves they don't know how to handle it, but as with all things practice makes perfect. An appraisal meeting is as good a time as any to start.

- Make it specific: identify clearly the action or behaviour you are praising.

- Give it as soon as possible after the event.

- Use positive words.

- Give it whenever it is deserved.

- Give it informally and repeat it formally.

- Show your pleasure in their success.

- Never mix praise with criticism – there is always a danger that the praise will be perceived as being insincere and is being used only to soften the criticism

- Keep your visual and verbal behaviour in harmony.

AT THE END OF THE APPRAISAL MEETING

The vast majority of appraisal meetings are highly successful – the appraisee leaves, feeling that they have had an opportunity to express their views and have been listened to, while the appraiser feels that they have deepened their understanding of the appraisee and have created a basis for more effective management. One important element of the process which must not be overlooked in achieving this success, however, is how the meeting is brought to a conclusion.

At the end of the appraisal meeting:

- Make every effort to resolve any disagreements.

- Agree actions – objectives, training and any other plans.

- Summarise, so that both parties understand what has been agreed.

- Confirm what will happen next.

- Both parties should sign the form.

- End on a positive note.

FOLLOW-UP ACTION AFTER THE MEETING

Action required after the appraisal meeting will depend on the specific requirements of the system being used. Most, however, will require some follow-up action for the appraiser before the process is finished.

This may include:

- putting on paper for the appraisee a clear statement of the objectives which have been agreed;

- making recommendations to the appropriate people about training and development requirements;

- passing the appraisal form to the 'grandparent' for comment;

- taking copies of the form for the personnel file;

- sending the completed form to the central administration.

Chapter 10

TRAINING AND SKILL DEVELOPMENT FOR APPRAISERS

The skills required by an appraiser are similar to those which are currently – and which will increasingly be – required by all managers in the future. Back in the mid-1980s Tom Peters and Bob Waterman wrote *In Search of Excellence*, suggesting that the key management skills for the future would be more concerned with coaching and helping than with directing and controlling. In 1994, a survey of British managers published in *The Observer* newspaper identified 'the ability to lead and adapt to change, to motivate staff and to work in a creative fashion' as being the most important management skills required in the 1990s.

Many people have argued for a long time that everyone at work has greater potential than they have been allowed to realise and that the contribution they could make to the success of the organisation would be enhanced if they were encouraged to take more ownership for what they do. The missing factor in bringing this situation about has, unfortunately, been a lack of skill in many managers to cope with a more responsible, self-managed workforce. Of course, it is true to say that a great many managers, in all sorts of organisations, disprove this view daily. Unfortunately, however, although they exist, they are not yet in the majority in many organisations.

Working in a wide cross section of organisations during the last few years has persuaded me that for every manager who listens to – and hears – the exhortations of the trainer to spend more time coaching, to learn to walk as they talk, to show a genuine interest in their people and so on, there are two who either fail to hear, or lack the skills to bring about the changes necessary. The skills required in managing people, in leading, motivating, communicating and in building teams, are more conspicuous by their absence than their presence in most organisations. This is one of the main reasons why many managers find the whole process of appraisal difficult. They lack the skills required to enable them to sit down and engage in an open and honest discussion with the people who report to them.

It is helpful to look at the skills required in appraisal at two levels, although there is some overlap. Firstly, there are general, people-handling skills which, if the manager has them, will make the appraisal easier to handle. Secondly, there are the more specific skills required in effective appraisal. It is not the purpose of this report to review management skills as a whole – this has been done elsewhere and is the subject of many books and training courses. It is just worth saying that the manager who generally adopts an open, empowering style, who takes trouble with communication and demonstrates a genuine interest in people, will in all probability find appraisal easier and will therefore do it better.

THE KEY SKILLS IN APPRAISAL

The key skills which are required in appraisal are:

- building rapport;

- questioning;

- listening;

- giving feedback.

We will now look at each of these in more detail.

BUILDING RAPPORT

Establishing rapport is about getting on the same wavelength as another person, tuning in, getting a meeting of more than minds, a meeting of whole persons. Of course, the rational side of things, like a meeting of minds, may occur in any case, but it is far more likely to happen – and more quickly – when rapport has been established. When we meet someone for the first time, or when we meet someone again after a gap, or even when we meet with someone we know well but are meeting them in a different context, establishing rapport is important.

Once we have established rapport through getting the emotional and feelings elements of our interactions in tune, the rational elements of our interactions will begin to work more easily and effectively. Communication frequently breaks down when little or no effort has been made to establish rapport and people launch into potentially contentious discussion or nego-tiation without getting onto the most appropriate wavelength to start with. One could almost say that establishing rapport is an essential prerequisite to effective communication.

When we meet someone for the first time, or when we meet someone in a new, different, perhaps more formal context, our senses go into overdrive to process all the data we are pre-sented with. The data we have to process is everything that is available to us about the other person. If it is a first time meeting we use the appearance, presentation, handshake, tone of voice and what they have to say as our first indicators. We take all of this information in via all of our senses, process it quickly and reach some initial conclusions. These generally cover such things as whether we like or dislike, should we trust or distrust, and all of the many other things we assess during the first minutes (seconds) of a meeting.

In much the same way, when we meet a familiar person in a new context we have to take in, process and assess any new data. In the context of an appraisal interview, both parties are in a new unfamiliar situation. Any changes in the environment, the atmosphere, the behaviour of the other person, will have to be processed and assessed. The more effectively the appraiser handles this early stage of the meeting, the more likely it is that rapport will be established and the meeting will get off to a good start.

When rapport has been established it leads to a much greater sensitivity to the needs and feelings of the other person, to much greater understanding and chance of agreement between both parties.

Techniques for establishing rapport

There are a number of things we can to do to help us establish rapport; some of them come naturally to many people. We all have acquaintances whom we recognise as always seeming to get on well with other people. In these cases it is likely that these people use some simple techniques for building rapport.

- **Non-threatening small talk**. This is a useful starting point – we can use it to establish or recall some shared experience. Having something to share allows us to gently probe for common experiences which we can agree about. It might be a programme on the TV last night, the weather, or the journey to work that morning. What we are seeking to do is to find a topic about which we can agree, where the other person can meet you half way and feel comfortable with the topic. What we are actually doing is to get to a position where we feel comfortable with each other. Establishing agreement about small things will enable us more easily to reach agreement about larger, more important things later. If the small talk we engage in can be of a humorous or lighthearted nature we add an additional element in establishing rapport. Humour can play an important part, but it is difficult to get right, and because of this has to be handled with care.

- **Using compatible behaviours**. Our behaviour, the way we act, the way we speak, even the words we use, can have a great influence on how we establish relationships with other people. This works when we mirror the behaviour of the other person. Mirroring behaviour is the practice of using the same behaviours as the person you are interacting with. We can see this most clearly through our visual behaviour – the way we sit, the way we cross, or don't cross, our legs or our arms, the way we use our hands, using the same facial expressions as the other person, all can have a significant influence on how the other person relates to us. An example which we are all familiar with is the smile – when someone we meet greets us with a genuine smile, an almost unconscious reaction is for us to smile back. This is a classic example of mirroring behaviour. You can test how effectively you have established rapport by deliberately mirroring the behaviour of another person; after a few minutes of doing this, make a change to your behaviour and see if the other person follows. A simple shift, like crossing or uncrossing your legs, will be sufficient to test how well you have established rapport – if the other person follows your behaviour you can safely assume that you have established rapport.

- **Using the other person's name**. The sound of our name is a powerful attention getter, and it influences how we perceive the person using it. Using the other person's name in an appropriate way early on in an interaction helps establish rapport. Appropriate use refers to the use of the name, fitting the context. An inappropriate use would be where people generally refer to each other in a formal way, using Miss, Mr or Mrs when addressing each other, then thinking that in a particular situation – perhaps a social event, or even an appraisal – it would help to get on first name terms. This is unlikely to work. Those people who have been on the receiving end of this will tell you that it does not help rapport. In fact the reverse may even be the case, as it frequently leads to difficulty and embarrassment. Equally, to use someone's name in an over-familiar or a mechanical way can create more problems than it solves.

- **Empathy.** Empathy is of course an important way of establishing rapport. Empathy is the ability we demonstrate to see things from the other person's point of view, how far you can put yourself into the other person's shoes, and both see and feel the situation from their perspective. Empathy does not work if we feel it but keep our feelings to ourselves. It is essential to demonstrate it if it is to work for us.

QUESTIONING

The ability to ask appropriate questions is important because the appraisal meeting should be an opportunity for the manager to get to know more about the views, feelings and opinions of the person being appraised. If the appraiser does all the talking this will not happen, and if inappropriate questions are asked the appraiser will end up doing all the talking.

The appraiser also has to keep the process moving and ensure that the focus remains on those issues which are important to them. Every effort must be made to help the appraisee explore issues and deepen their understanding. Without effective questions none of this will happen.

The words used in framing a question are important, but it is equally important not to overlook the manner in which they are asked. An atmosphere of openness and trust has to be created and this will only happen if questions are asked in a sensitive manner.

A strategy for questions

We use questions for different reasons. It is useful to review these reasons, as some are more helpful than others, especially as we use them in appraisal. The following are some of the more important:

- To explore an issue – *'What do you think of that?'*
- To get ideas – *'How can we solve this?'*
- To get information – *'Which out of these do you find most interesting?'*
- To check for agreement – *'Do you agree with?'*
- To seek clarification – *'Can you explain that a little more?'*
- To get an opinion – *'What do you think of?'*
- To get a reaction – *'What would you do if...?'*
- To identify needs – *'What would you find most helpful?'*

Each of these can be used in appraisal but the appraiser, in preparing for the meeting, should think about which to use and how to use them.

Patterns of questioning

We can identify two main approaches to how an appraiser can use questions: the choice is to either start narrow and move to broader issues or start broad and move to consideration of more specific issues. These approaches are often described as the pyramid and the funnel.

Pyramid

This approach starts by focusing on specific issues first and then broadening out to consider some broader ones. The pyramid pattern can be useful in allowing the appraisee to focus their mind and concentration on some specific aspects of performance, and after discussion of this move out to a consideration of broader issues.

Funnel

This approach works from the opposite direction and starts broad and becomes narrow. It can be used to approach difficult issues in a more gentle way as it allows the discussion to develop towards a more specific focus.

Both approaches are equally valid and can be used interchangeably.

Types of question

Many different types of question have been identified and we will describe a number of the types most appropriate to appraisal.

Open ended questions

Perhaps, the most famous description of open ended questions is given in the Rudyard Kipling poem:

> *I had my six good serving men,*
> *they taught me all I knew,*
> *their names were,*
> *how and why and what*
> *and when and where and who.*

A question beginning with any of these words is more likely to result in an answer giving more information than just a yes or no. Open ended questions are generally designed to open up an issue, they seek to explore feelings and thoughts behind issues and to do this they have to get the other person talking.

In addition to the six words above, open ended questions may begin with the appraiser saying, *'Tell me about ...?'*, or something similar, the purpose being to get the other person to open up.

Closed questions

This type of question should be used sparingly as it is designed to elicit short answers such as a *yes* or a *no*. If the appraiser relies overmuch on such questions it is likely that the appraiser will be doing too much of the talking. They can be phrased as:

- *'Did you do that ...?'*

- *'Have you done this ...?'*

- *'Has this been completed ...?'*

Linking questions

These are used for linking back to something which the appraisee has said earlier. Their use demands that the appraiser listen attentively.

- *'You said earlier that ... How do you think it could ...?'*

High value questions

Most business situations have some time constraints and, while time should not be a major consideration in appraisal, it cannot be ignored. If time is becoming a problem during an appraisal, the high value question can help to focus the mind of both parties on the important issues. This type of question is designed to help identify priorities.

- *'We have now identified eight possible ... Which two of these would you like to concentrate on?'*

Comparative questions

These can be used to compare a situation, perhaps on a before and after basis.

- *'How has your experience of ... affected your attitude to ...?'*

- *'What have you done since ...?'*

Hypothetical questions

These can be designed to allow the appraisee to explore issues in a safe way, without having to make a commitment.

- *'How would you feel about ...?'*

- *'What would you do if ...?'*

Permission questions

Frequently used in counselling, they allow the appraiser to test how the appraisee feels about further, deeper, discussion on a topic which may be sensitive or personal.

- *'How do you feel about discussing ...?'*

Questions which extend

When the appraiser wants to probe a little deeper, or prompt for further information, a question which extends the discussion may help.

- *'That's interesting. Tell me a little more ...'*
- *'How else would you do ...?'*

All of the above are useful types of question, which can aid the progress of the appraisal meeting. There are, however, also some types of question which it is better to avoid in an appraisal situation.

Leading questions

These are often called *loaded questions* as the question actually contains within it the expected answer. To do this is contrary to good appraisal practice, as it attempts to put words into the mouth of the appraisee, forgetting that the purpose of appraisal is to get the appraisee to express their own views.

- *'Do you agree that ...?'*
- *'I believe that ... What do you think?'*
- *'You don't really believe that, do you?'*

Multiple questions

Questions which actually contain more than one question can lead to confusion and uncertainty in the appraisee.

- *'Why do you ... How will it ... Can you see an alternative ...?'*

It is important to avoid asking too many questions as it can create a feeling that the meeting is more like an interrogation than an appraisal. Also avoid probing too deeply unless you have sought permission to do so beforehand.

Techniques to support questions

The important thing about an appraisal is that it should flow easily from one subject area to the next without too much hesitation and without becoming stilted. This can be helped by use of some simple techniques.

- **Paraphrasing** can be used to to help the appraiser clarify what the appraisee means or even to enable to appraisee to amend or adjust what they are saying. The process is for the appraiser to repeat in their own words what the appraisee has just said. This allows the appraisee to check the meaning, and the appraiser to check their understanding.

- **Reflecting back**, like paraphrasing, is a technique which enables the appraisee to listen to what they have said and provides an opportunity for clarification or change. The appraiser might say: *'So what I understand you to be saying is ...?'*

- **Summarising** should happen at the end of each main section and involves a short résumé of what has been agreed so far.

LISTENING

The best, most well structured approach to questioning that can be imagined will come to nothing if the questioner does not listen to the answers. An essential skill for appraisers is the ability to listen; if an appraiser cannot listen it will not be possible to conduct an effective appraisal. There is a saying that *'We have two ears and one mouth and the appraiser should use them in these proportions.'*

We have a tendency to believe that listening is easy – after all, it is something we do all of the time, so why do we need to give it special attention? Many believe that listening is a passive activity when, in fact, effective listening requires the active involvement of the listener. Unfortunately, the skill of listening is deficient in many managers. For others, pressed as they are for time and with so many priorities and things to do, it is something which gets overlooked.

An important element in listening is the behaviour we use, both verbal and non-verbal.

Verbal behaviours which support listening

- The use of verbal prompts such as, *'Um-hum'*, *'Ye-e-s'*, *'I see'*, *'Go on'*.

- The use of additional information gaining questions, *'Can you tell me a bit more about that?'*

- The use of a tone of voice which is relaxed and rational.

Non-verbal behaviours which support listening

- Eye contact is perhaps the most important way of communicating attention to the other person. It is easily achieved by making sure that you focus your eyes on the other person for about 60% of the time

- By nodding our head at appropriate times we can communicate attention.

- Using appropriate facial expressions. Our facial expression should reflect our feelings – pleasure at the success of the other person; quizzical when posing a question or seeking a more detailed answer; perhaps a frown when we don't understand.

- Using an open body posture. This means uncrossed arms and legs – unless, of course, you are mirroring the behaviour of the appraisee. But even if this is the case, you should be mirroring them in order to lead them into a more open posture.

- Leaning into the discussion. Leaning forward, towards the other person, communicates interest and attention.

- Don't assume you know what they are going to say. Avoid dismissive gestures such as waving your hands to imply you already know that, or nodding your head to communicate no.

Effective listening demands attention and concentration. The following checklist will help you to keep on track.

Checklist for effective questioning and listening

- Be prepared to sit out awkward silences.
- Give the appraisee time to find the right words.
- Don't assume you know what they are going to say, even if this means a few seconds of silence.
- Keep clarifying and summarising.
- Avoid asking leading questions.
- Ask one question at a time.
- Be a conscientious listener.
- Don't show boredom or irritation.
- Maintain your concentration.

GIVING FEEDBACK

We have already stated that a primary purpose of appraisal is to improve performance, and from this it must follow that we can only improve what we know is deficient. The way we find out what we can improve is through feedback. In many ways feedback is the basis of all learning. Without knowing how well you have done it is almost impossible to imagine that you could seek to improve. For the effective manager the ability to give feedback is an essential skill, to be used during appraisal but also to be used in the day-to-day activity of managing and leading people.

The manager is sometimes reluctant to give feedback for fear of appearing to be condescending or for fear of being hurtful. This often means that many people have little or no idea about how they are doing. Our ability to give feedback improves with practice, so if we are really concerned to raise the performance of our people, we need to let them know how they are doing.

Feedback is also a way of learning more about ourselves and the effect our behaviour has on other people. Giving feedback can increase our self-awareness, identify options for change and contribute to our self-development.

When giving feedback we should always aim to make it constructive. Constructive feedback does not mean that it should only cover good news – negative feedback given skilfully is equally important in the way in which it contributes to the development of the other person. Given in an unskilled way, negative feedback can be destructive.

The following guidelines will help you to give constructive feedback.

Guidelines for constructive feedback

- Give feedback as soon as possible after the event.

- Be clear what you want to say in advance. Rehearse or write down the key points.

- Check that the other person understands what you are saying, by asking them to restate or rephrase what you have said.

- Own the feedback, i.e. begin with an 'I' statement such as *'I heard'* or *'I saw'*. This indicates that you realise you are expressing your own personal view and are aware other people may think differently.

- Start with the positive.

- Select priority areas to cover. Don't give too much feedback at any one time.

- Be specific.

- Focus on the behaviour or the action, not on the person.

- Be descriptive rather than evaluative.

- Offer alternatives – give examples of what could have been done differently.

- Think what the feedback is saying about you.

DEVELOPING THE SKILLS

It is one thing to describe the techniques and another to develop them. As was said above, there are many books and training courses which can help to give a greater insight into these skills. An appraisal training course will spend time considering some of these issues and developing the skills, but managers need to take action themselves to build their own skills.

The most obvious thing you can do to develop your skills is to practise. Of course, you will not always get it right first time but it is more important to try and perhaps not end up with a perfect result than not to try at all. Once you have tried something it is always easier to do it again and improve your performance each time, through personal reflection and by seeking feedback from others.

A TYPICAL TRAINING COURSE OUTLINE

Training for appraisers is essential, and is something that organisations fail to do at their peril. The length and detail of the course will vary, depending on the specific requirements of individual organisations. An important element to include, however, is the provision of some time to practise carrying out an appraisal. Many people have little or no idea what to expect from an appraisal interview and the experience of seeing it done during a training course can be really helpful.

Participants in training courses, although they may dislike the idea of role playing, often remark that seeing an interview take place is the most useful part of the course.

The following course outline is based on two full days training during normal working hours – approximately fourteen hours training – for twelve people. This course assumes that a rating system and objective setting will be used as part of the appraisal.

If it is to be effective, the course needs to be informal, flexible, highly participative and responsive to the needs of the delegates.

Course objectives

Upon completion of the course participants will:

- understand the background to the appraisal system;
- understand the benefits of appraisal for the individual, the manager and the organisation;
- understand how appraisal will work in the organisation;
- have identified potential pitfalls and difficulties and discussed ways to overcome these;
- understand and be able to apply the rating system;
- be equipped to set measurable objectives for their staff;
- have developed and practised appraisal interviewing skills.

Day one

Course introduction, objectives and expectations

- It is important to get participants to state their expectations and concerns. The trainer can note these and make sure they are addressed during the course.

Appraisal systems purpose and benefits

- A syndicate discussion to get participants thinking about the purpose and benefits of appraisal for:
  - the organisation;
  - the manager;
  - the individual employee.

- The discussion should also cover the specific benefits they believe their organisation, managers and employees will get out of appraisal.

The appraisal system outlined

- A detailed explanation of the appraisal system. The form, the process, the timetable and other practical details of the system should be outlined.

How to use the rating scale

- An introduction followed by a discussion and practical exercise on completing a sample rating scale.

How to set objectives

- An explanation of the process to be used for setting objectives should outline what an objective is and introduce techniques for setting objectives.
- A practical exercise in setting objectives. This should get participants to identify real people and try setting objectives for them. When groups report back, the objectives they have set should be critically analysed and feedback provided.

Skills and techniques in appraisal interviewing

- Preparation for appraisal.
- The setting for appraisal.
- The structure for appraisal.
- Conducting the interview.

Day two

Role play

- Time constraints may make it difficult for all participants to take part in a role play at this stage. The basic requirement must be to show one complete appraisal interview through a series of roles plays.
- A useful way of doing this is to split the interview into three separate sections as follows and hold three role plays:
  - introduction and rating of performance;
  - discussion of and setting of objectives for the next period;
  - personal development, potential and aspirations, and final summary.

Developing interview skills

- Session to cover the key interview skills including:

  – building rapport;

  – questioning;

  – listening;

  – giving feedback.

Role play in trios

- A second role play to involve all participants working in trios. Participants take it in turn to play the role of appraiser, appraisee and observer. The observer gives feedback to the others after each role play. It helps if the roles being played can be as close as possible to the reality of the participants. This can be done by asking participants to prepare a pen picture of an appraisee they will have to appraise, briefing their partner and asking the partner to play this role.

- Ample time has to be allowed for this exercise – for a course of twelve people this exercise will require approximately one and one half hours. To try to do it in less will significantly reduce the benefit.

Questions we might expect

- Syndicate discussion to identify typical questions which people will ask about the appraisal system. The questions identified should be recorded on flip charts and during the report back, questions posed by one group should be answered by another, supported by the trainer as necessary.

Plenary session to answer final questions

- An opportunity to ask questions which have not been covered.

Personal action plans

- Delegates to prepare their own action plans.

Chapter 11

TRAINING FOR APPRAISEES

In an organisation which is introducing a system of appraisal for the first time there will be a lot of uncertainty and apprehension among the people who are going to be appraised. Appraisal holds fears for many people who may feel that it is designed to provide the boss with reasons for telling them off, perhaps even to discover reasons to get rid of them. Unfortunately, for many people, appraisal is seen as a negative and threatening experience, rather than what it is intended to be, a positive motivating experience.

Even for those who don't fear appraisal, but who are experiencing it for the first time, uncertainty about what it means and how it operates may mean that it will not deliver to expectations. Unless people are clear about it, appraisal will frequently be viewed with suspicion. People need to know what it involves, how it operates, what their role will be and, above all, what is the purpose of it.

The introduction of appraisal also results not infrequently in raising a whole series of new expectations in employees. This is generally a positive outcome but one which needs to be planned for and handled well once these expectations have been identified and articulated. The type of expectations which are raised can include greater access to training opportunities, increased opportunity for promotion and/or regrading, an expectation that in future management will listen more closely to their concerns and recognise how hard they work.

The introduction of performance related pay can result in many people believing that pay levels will be raised across the board. Most people believe that they deliver a good level of performance and are, therefore, worth more than they currently get. This leads them to believe that with pay now being related to performance, they can reasonably expect to get an increase. This situation is perfectly understandable as it is very likely they will not previously have been told how performance is measured, or perhaps even how their performance is seen and rated by their manager.

There are, as we have seen in Chapter 1, significant benefits to be gained from appraisal. Appraisal, however, is not a panacea, and the benefits to be gained, however important, will not extend to meeting the personal needs of all employees.

All of these expectations have to be managed positively if the appraisal is to be successful. It is in the interests of all that the appraisal is seen to be a motivating experience. If, however, the early exposure to it raises expectations, only to have them dashed, getting it back on track as a motivating experience becomes more difficult.

The way to do this most effectively is to make sure that the communications and training process is well planned and effective. A plan for communication was given in Chapter 5.

Equally important is the role which can be played by training in overcoming the fears and uncertainties, and ensuring that expectations are managed and the benefits to be gained from appraisal are achieved for the employees and the organisation.

Details of a short training session for appraisees is outlined below.

TRAINING SESSION OUTLINE

A typical training session for appraisees should be scheduled to last for about three to four hours and should seek to cover all of the main elements of the appraisal. Ample time should also be allowed for people to ask questions – in fact this should be actively encouraged.

Session objectives

- To introduce the new appraisal process to all employees.
- To explain and discuss the objectives and purpose of our appraisal process.
- To outline how the system will work.
- To discuss the role of the appraisee.
- To answer questions about the process.

Welcome and introduction

- Welcome and scene setting.
- Objectives and expectations for the session.
- Why are we introducing appraisal?
- Appraisal objectives.
- The benefits of appraisal (should cover the WIIFM, 'What's in it for me?').

Syndicate exercise

Working in small groups, participants should be asked to explore:
- what they understand by appraisal;
- what they would like to get out of appraisal;
- what they believe their role to be;
- any fears or concerns they may identify.

The appraisal process outlined

- An outline of how the system will operate.
- The form to be used.

- How the assessment will work.
- Ensuring fairness and equity.
- The proposed timetable.
- Administration.

The role of the appraisee

- The management expectation of you.
- Self appraisal – how it works.
- Personal development – what do you want to achieve?
- Your part in planning for your appraisal.
- Your part in the appraisal interview.

Buzz groups

Small groups should be formed to identify any questions which have not been covered which can then be posed in a neutral way by the group rather than an individual.

Session close

The person presenting the session should make sure that the session closes on a high note. It is important to make sure that participants leave the session feeling that appraisal will be a positive experience and that they have much to gain from it.

Chapter 12

THE PITFALLS AND POTENTIAL BARRIERS TO PERFORMANCE APPRAISAL

A key concern for managers thinking about introducing a system for performance appraisal will be to identify the pitfalls and barriers which may get in the way of a successful introduction. It has to be said that there are pitfalls awaiting the unwary and anyone who has ever worked in the field of performance appraisal will acknowledge that barriers exist. There will always be someone around to tell you *'it won't work here because ...'*

The key of course is to identify potential problems and plan to overcome them. We will look first at the potential pitfalls which can, pretty well always, be put down to a failure to anticipate and plan for some element or other. The barriers, on the other hand, are those forces in the organisation which are working against successful implementation.

PITFALLS

As indicated above, the potential pitfalls are almost all avoidable with careful thinking and planning as they are usually caused by problems in the design of the system or in the communication and training which precedes introduction. The checklist which follows should be seen as a problem-solving checklist which can be consulted in the event of an organisation identifying problems with their performance appraisal system. All of the problems identified in the list can be overcome or avoided if careful attention is paid to the advice given throughout this report.

The causes of common problems with appraisal systems

If problems exist with an appraisal system, the following checklist may help you to identify why and point towards a possible solution.

- The organisation has failed to agree clearly defined objectives for the introduction of a system of performance appraisal.

- There is a misunderstanding at senior management level as to the purposes of appraisal.

- There are mixed expectations of what the system will deliver.

- There is a lack of clarity about what the system will relate to and what will be included. For example, will there be a direct relationship to pay, and if so, has this been clearly built into the operation of the system?

- The system may be based on the use of both a rating scale and setting objectives, but be unclear about which of these should take precedence when assessing performance.

- The criteria for evaluating performance may not have been thoroughly researched and agreed.

- There may be a lack of clarity about who will be appraised and who will do the appraising.

- Systems may not have been created to ensure effective central administration which can provide support and information.

- Line managers may not have been involved sufficiently in the design of the system which may therefore meet their resistance.

- Managers may fail to own the system which will be seen as belonging to the personnel or human resources department.

- Employee representatives may not have been involved and consulted which results in their resistance.

- The communications process supporting the introduction of the system may have been inadequate leading to confusion, fear and misapprehension.

- The managers doing the appraisals do not properly understand why they are doing them. This means that the appraisal meetings will not be conducted to best effect.

- Appraisers may not have received adequate training leading to the appraisal meetings being badly conducted. This in turn has the effect of destroying employees' confidence in the system.

- Appraisees have not received any training leading to fear, mistrust and lack of confidence in the system.

- There is no clear process for resolving disputes between appraisers and appraisees, the result of which is to create all round dissatisfaction.

THE BARRIERS TO PERFORMANCE APPRAISAL

In considering the barriers which may exist, it is useful to look at them as originating from two different perspectives: as coming from the culture or environmental factors in the organisation, and as originating with individuals in the organisation.

Organisational barriers

The type of cultural barriers which can get in the way of appraisal can generally be put down to issues of management style and organisation structure. It may be that the atmosphere in the organisation is not conducive to the most effective use of a system of appraisal. Of course, this does not mean that an appraisal system could not be introduced, only that it would be less likely to deliver the results as they have been described in this report.

Appraisal systems have been in use in many organisations for a very long time. They were introduced in some instances as an extension of the process of management control. In organisations where the dominant style was one of directing and controlling employees, appraisal was frequently used as a once-a-year way of telling employees what the manager – and through **him**, what the organisation – thought of them. In these circumstances there was little involvement and very likely no attempt at self-appraisal. The perceived view, however, may well have been that once a year it was a good thing to tell the 'troops' what was thought of them.

This type of system may very well have worked satisfactorily within the social and cultural setting in which it was placed. It is, however, unlikely to work now and may even be counter-productive.

The way we judge an effective appraisal system now will be very different to how it would have been judged in the past. As organisations become more open and seek to empower and in-volve the workforce, the appraisal system, as a key element in the management and employee interchange, needs to be appropriate to the overall culture and style of the organisation.

To overcome this problem, if it exists, requires that the organisation understand its culture, and perhaps, in seeking to change it, appraisal can be one of the drivers for cultural change.

It is also true that in an organisation that is divided, perhaps between operations and support services, appraisal will be more difficult. Of course, many, if not most, organisations exhibit some division between operations and support but most learn to live and cope with the division. The concern for appraisal is in those few organisations where the division is real and often encouraged from the top. Appraisal will not act as a means of healing – it may in fact exaggerate the divisions and is best not introduced in these circumstances.

As part of a package of measures designed to change the culture it may well have an important role to play. It is a highly effective means of communicating, but only when all of the appraisers are singing from the same hymn sheet.

Organisations which are seeking to use appraisal as part of a package of measures to achieve change would be well advised to consider not just appraisal on its own, but the whole question of performance management.

Barriers in people

It is tempting to say that the barriers in people can be traced to two main sources, namely:

- lack of trust;
- lack of skill.

So what does this mean and how does it manifest itself?

Lack of trust can permeate throughout the whole organisation – employees don't trust management and managers don't trust the senior management group, or perhaps more commonly the personnel department who are the originators of the system. Where this exists, it is likely to show itself in the following ways:

- a belief that the system is inherently unfair;
- participation with reluctance;
- cynicism;
- lack of interest/commitment;
- resistance to the process;
- not committing the time necessary to make it a success;
- not operating the system fairly at a local level;
- employees and managers working actively to undermine the process.

All of these barriers can be overcome by senior management making a strenuous effort to involve and consult line management at all levels in making sure that the system is fair, equitable and relevant.

If key decisions about appraisal, the process to be used, how assessments are made and so on are taken behind closed doors, then it is inevitable that there will be a lack of trust in the system. The point was made in Chapter 1 that appraisal has to be owned by the line management who have a responsibility to make sure that it is seen to be as fair as it can be made.

Lack of skill is, of course, easier to deal with than lack of trust, but first of all it has to be acknowledged. In far too many organisations it is assumed that if you are a manager you are automatically capable of appraising. In fact conducting an appraisal meeting is difficult for even the most experienced and effective manager.

Lack of skill can also be a problem where the appraisee is concerned, although here perhaps a lack of knowledge would be a better description.

Lack of knowledge and skill lead to:

- inadequate preparation;
- poor information giving;
- fear of close interaction with appraisees;
- badly handled meetings;
- poorly set objectives ;
- appraisee demotivated as a result of the meeting;
- performance rating scores not thought through, leading to disagreements;
- inadequate briefing for appraisees.

The solution to these problems and to others of a similar nature is to make sure that the introduction of a new appraisal system, or even following a review and redesign of an existing system, is accompanied by a well planned communications programme as outlined in Chapter 5. The same point can be applied to the development of skills for both appraisers and appraisees and training programmes as outlined in Chapters 10 and 11.

In many ways the success of an appraisal system can be boiled down to three key issues. Get these right and you are much more likely to succeed:

- **the design of the system, the process and form;**

- **the supporting communications programme;**

- **the quality of the training provided.**

CONCLUSIONS

Does appraisal work?

Over the years much has been written and said about performance appraisal and views vary widely about its effectiveness as a way of achieving improved performance. Talking to managers, employees and human resource specialists in a wide range of organisations leads me to believe that few are entirely happy with the process used in their organisation. The reasons for this dissatisfaction are varied and include perceived problems with the design of the forms being used, its relevance to the needs of the managers and employees being appraised and in some cases the bureaucratic requirements of the the central administration.

In some cases the problems raised are related to a lack of clarity about the requirements and objectives of the process. Frequently, where the process was related to a system of perform-ance related pay this is perceived to create additional problems. It would seem that we have not yet come to terms with the idea that pay and performance should be related, or perhaps it is because we have not yet developed systems which people feel do this in a satisfactory way.

A further issue raised by some was the perceived difficulty of handling, in a satisfactory manner, the appraisal meeting. Appraisal meetings seem to be awkward occasions which interfere with the normal interaction between manager and employee, the behaviours used being false – such as when the manager sits outside the desk because this is what he or she has been told to do at the training course. This, it is claimed, makes both the manager and the appraisee feel uncomfortable.

Appraisal, it seems, poses new difficulties for people which require them to behave in a way which is different to the way they normally behave in relation to each other. Of course this must pose some serious questions about the normal interaction and behaviour between managers and the people who report to them. If it is not usually conducted on an adult, rational plane, then the behaviours required at appraisal will seem false. These behaviours, however, are those which should characterise the normal behaviours which adults engage in, even if there is a boss–subordinate relationship. So perhaps this particular group of critics of appraisal need to understand that the behaviour required at appraisal should be the norm. It is other behaviour, especially if it seeks to place one person in a controlling position and the other in a submissive role, which is false. Having open, honest relationships is essential to working effectively together.

Interestingly, however, most of the people referred to above who live in doubt about the benefits of appraisal, when challenged, are unable to come up with an alternative which could do better in terms of achieving the primary purpose of appraisal. This essentially can be defined as:

An exploration between the appraiser and appraisee of how well the appraisee did during the previous months, how this performance can be improved and what objectives can be set for the next period.

When the focus is placed on the aims of appraisal most agree that appraisal is perhaps the best way of achieving the outcomes required. This is not to say that the majority feel that the systems they currently use are perfect – far from it, but they do feel that without some form of regular appraisal any prospect of assessing performance and encouraging improvement would be immensely more difficult.

Where this points us, I believe, is to the conclusion that appraisal is an important management technique which sometimes fails to live up to the expectations we have of it. Rather than suggest that appraisal doesn't work and therefore we should get rid of it as a means of assessing and improving performance, we need to renew our efforts in making it more effective. We can start this process by reviewing what we are currently doing in the light of what our objectives for appraisal are.

Conducting an audit

The first step in this process is to audit the system which is currently in use. This should identify and highlight any problems which exist and point towards the ways in which we can overcome them. Of course, it may lead us to the conclusion that the best solution would be to conduct a complete root and branch review of the system currently in use. If this is required we should do it in much the same way as we would plan the introduction of a process of appraisal if one didn't already exist. The first step, however, is the audit.

In conducting the audit it is essential that the users, both appraisers and appraisees, are fully involved and that their views are listened to and acted upon. A suggested approach could be as follows.

- Design and conduct a survey to assess management and staff opinion. Many employee attitude surveys already ask some questions about appraisal but it is important to remember that this survey is only about appraisal. It is unlikely that you will get sufficient information from a couple of questions added into a more general survey.

- It is not necessary to survey every employee – a representative sample should be sufficient to provide the information you require. Given the sensitive nature of the information and a possible reluctance on the part of employees to respond to a survey conducted

103

through internal resources, it may be advisable to commission an external consultancy to conduct the survey. Doing this gives employees a greater sense of confidentiality.

- A survey will provide a lot of information about what people think and suggestions for improvement. To gain real benefits, however, requires a further step, that of building on the information gained through a series of interviews with managers and focus groups with employees. These face-to-face discussions allow you to probe and explore many of the 'how to' and 'what if' questions which will have been raised as a result of the survey.

- In designing the survey and follow-up discussions, it will be important to cover not only the perceived problems with the current system but what people would put in its place. The interviews and focus groups will allow you to explore issues such as upward appraisal, peer appraisal and 360 degree appraisal.

Once the survey and follow-up work has been completed you will have available a lot of information on which to build a new approach to appraisal. Whatever type of appraisal you decide to develop, it will be important to ensure that it is owned by line management and this can only be achieved if they are involved in the design. There is, of course, a role for the personnel specialist, who can bring insight, knowledge and professional experience to bear on the process. The golden rule of ownership should be remembered – that is, if the appraisal is not owned by line management it will not be effective.

Developing a system for performance appraisal

A suggested process for the design or re-design of a system of appraisal could take the following steps.

Agree a clear purpose and aims for the system, the key questions being, *'Why do we want a system of appraisal and what do we want to get out of it?'*

Consideration of the following issues will help to focus this debate:

- Should the appraisal system have a role in determining pay?
- Total pay or just bonus?
- Should we have a strict system of performance related pay?
- Should the appraisal system assess the long-term potential of employees?
- Should development appraisal be separate from performance appraisal?
- Should the appraisal system include:
  - self-appraisal;
  - peer appraisal;
  - team appraisal;
  - upward appraisal;
  - 360 degree appraisal?

Once the purpose and aims are agreed it becomes possible to set clear and measurable objectives for achieving these aims. The key questions here are, *'What objectives do we need to set if we are to achieve these aims and how will we know when we have succeeded?'*

Having agreed the aims and objectives, a small team of people can begin to design a system and process which will most effectively deliver what is required. Questions to be asked and answered at this point should all relate back to the previously agreed aims and objectives but should be directed to the practical application of these. For example, if one of the aims is to relate performance to pay through the appraisal system, the questions will be *'How can we best do this? What have others done? What can we learn from their experience? What will work best for us?'*

As far as possible the process should be consultative, involving people from all areas of the business and all levels, the intention being to ensure that ownership remains with line management. The design of the system should follow the process outlined in Chapter 2 under the heading 'A formal system'. The detail given in this section and which any design or re-design of a system needs to include can be summarised as:

- a set of procedures which will outline the process to be followed;

- some form of central administration;

- a form to be completed;

- an agreed time to hold the appraisal.

Once all of the above has been done, the organisation can begin to develop a plan for implementation.

A plan for implementation

The implementation plan needs to cover:

- communications;

- training;

- timing.

A detailed plan for communications was outlined in Chapter 5 and if this is followed it will ensure that everyone is fully informed and aware of all that is going on. It will also help people to understand their role and what is expected of them.

The importance of training and the contribution it can make to the effective implementation of a new or redesigned system cannot be overstated. Not to provide training is to ask for failure at the outset. Any organisation which is not prepared to commit the necessary resources to the training of appraisers and appraisees should seriously question if they should be introducing a new or redesigning an existing appraisal system at all.

Detailed plans for training were outlined in Chapters 10 and 11. If these are adapted to the specific requirements of organisations and the broad concepts as outlined are followed through, the training needs of both appraisers and appraisees will be met.

Getting the timing right is frequently a problem for many organisations – a new or re-designed system is being prepared and half way through this process a decision is taken to introduce it three months early. There are, of course, always very good organisational reasons for doing this; however, it has to be said that many a good system failed because it didn't get the communications process or the training right as a result of being rushed into implementation.

There is no easy answer to this problem but clear plans which are agreed at the outset and which identify milestones, accountabilities and dependencies, i.e. X must happen before Y can happen, can help to show the importance of getting the sequence right. Getting things right at the outset can save a lot of difficulty and heartache later.

Some final thoughts

This concluding section opened by posing the question, *'Does appraisal work?'* The answer to this is, *'Yes, but sometimes imperfectly.'*

This report has sought to identify some of the reasons for the imperfections and to show how they can be overcome. The fundamental premise of the report is that no matter how good the system, if it is not accepted by the people who operate it, if they don't understand it and don't feel comfortable using it, if they don't see its relevance to them and don't see how it contributes to their effectiveness and the effectiveness of their teams, they will not use it well. This mismatch between the aspirations for the system and the application of it in practice is the most frequent reason for systems to fail to deliver what is expected of them.

It is not up to the designers of systems to cast blame saying, *'This is a great system, if only those people out there would use it properly.'* It is up to the designers of systems to ensure that they create systems which meet the needs of those people out there. They will do this best by involving the users and listening to what they have to say.

On the other hand, line managers, team leaders and all who are responsible for providing leadership in organisations should be concerned with improving performance. This cannot happen if people do not know how they are doing, what improved performance means for them, receive support in achieving improved performance and have clear performance standards and objectives to work to.

So while there is a clear demand for the designers of systems to come up with the best possible system for the job, there is also a clear requirement for line managers to demand a system which enables them to help their people to get a clear focus on how to improve their performance and development.

Any system which is not meeting these requirements is in need of urgent overhaul. Any system which has been in use for five years or more without a thorough review is unlikely to be meeting current needs and will be in urgent need of that overhaul. Change has been so rapid in the recent past that it is almost impossible to accept that a system to appraise and encourage performance improvement introduced five years or more ago can still be doing this effectively.

Appraisal does work and employees, managers and organisations can gain significant benefit from the effective application of appraisal. To achieve this requires that time and effort be spent, firstly in thinking about and designing a system which meets the needs of the organisation, and then in monitoring, reviewing and evaluating the system to ensure that it continues to meet those needs.

Appendix A

GUIDANCE NOTE FOR MANAGERS

Most organisations, when introducing an system of appraisal for the first time, find it useful to issue some guidance notes for managers and employees. This appendix, and Appendix B which follows, are given solely as an example of a typical set of guidance notes.

INTRODUCTION

Starting with effect from this year, every employee will have a full performance appraisal each year. The purpose of the performance appraisal is for each employee to have an opportunity to discuss his or her performance, progress and development needs with their immediate manager. The appraisal will provide the organisation and each individual with an opportunity to explore jointly any concerns and future developments about the individual or the organisation.

Appraisal is most effective when a full and frank exchange of views takes place between the manager and the individual and this is best achieved when the person conducting the appraisal is the immediate manager of the appraisee. This means that in some instances the appraisal will be conducted by supervisors. The closer the appraiser is to the work of the individual the more effective the appraisal will be, as it is rooted in the real work experience of both people. You should identify who in your area will conduct the appraisals and agree this with your divisional manager as soon as possible.

We have designed a training course for all appraisers and it is important that all attend so early identification of appraisers is essential. Anyone who does not attend the training course should not appraise. In addition to the training you need to make sure that all of your appraisers are fully briefed about the system and the objectives, and understand how the process works. They should be provided with a copy of this booklet and the employee guidance notes. You should check that they understand these documents, the use of the appraisal form and the nature of the appraisal interview. Any difficulties an appraiser may have in preparing for the interview or completing the form should be referred to the Personnel Department.

BEFORE THE INTERVIEW

Appraisals will take place during May each year and in April you will receive forms for all your staff. About two weeks before you intend to hold the interviews you should give a copy of the form together with the employee guidance notes to each person to be appraised. You should explain to the employee that you want the interview to be as frank and honest as possible. The appraisee also needs to understand that it is important that they complete the self-appraisal element of the form and give consideration to appropriate objectives for the next year. The completed form should be returned to you, at least one week before the interview, allowing you sufficient time to insert your rating scores and comments and to discuss your provisional scores with your manager. It is suggested that for this initial scoring you use a pencil, so showing the appraisee that the content of the interview could easily change your view on some of the factors.

Appraisers should forward their initial markings to their manager as soon as possible as it will be essential to exercise some control over the standard of appraisal marking to ensure, as far as possible, a consistent approach across as wide an area as possible. This initial review of scores by a senior manager will also assist in minimising the possibility of any conflict of opinion concerning the appraisal rating of an individual arising between the appraiser and senior manager after the appraisal interview.

Once reviewed by the manager's manager and following any changes that may have been agreed, the appraisal forms should be returned to the appraiser in order that the appraisal interviews can commence. We are working to a tight timetable so every effort should be made to make sure we keep to it.

THE INTERVIEW

Make sure that you allow adequate time for the interview and ensure privacy and no interruptions. You should promote informality and put the interviewee at ease. Staff should be encouraged to talk freely, both in supporting their self-appraisal mark and comments and in expressing general views. Where an appraisee is asked to accept that they have scored themselves too highly this should be handled sensitively and the appraisee should be given the opportunity to agree to a lower rating without too much loss of face.

It is essential that praise is given where it is due and any criticism given should be given in a constructive way. All employees should be made aware that the Company will, in general, give support to their relevant career aspirations. If the individual requests specific assistance during the interview then that assistance, if realistically possible, should be offered. Uppermost in your mind should be the belief that the appraisal interview is valuable to the individual in its own right, not just as a means of assessing performance.

If disagreements occur, every effort should be made to resolve them at the interview. If, after sufficient effort, agreement cannot be reached this should be made clear on the form and the form signed by the appraisee, who may also write alongside the signature 'Read but not agreed'.

As you reach agreement on the ratings at the interview you should ink in your scores and at the end ask the appraisee to sign the form. If you decide to postpone completing the form to allow for some reconsideration of scores you will need to arrange another short meeting to tell the appraisee of your decision. If employees wish, they should be given a copy of the completed appraisal form.

The appraisal form will be a written record of the performance of each individual during the year and employees will need to be assured that the form will be treated with great confidentiality and that the contents will only be seen by those people with responsibility for furthering the careers of staff.

AFTER THE INTERVIEW

The completed appraisal forms should be sent to the appraiser's manager for review and completion of the final part of the form. If the appraiser's manager disagrees with the overall performance ratings given this should be discussed between the two parties concerned. If after this discussion the original ratings are revised the appraisee should be notified.

Although it is to be hoped that any disagreements will be resolved at the appraisal interview or shortly after, an appeals procedure has been established to hear grievances and all employees have a right to appeal if they do not agree with the final result of the appraisal.

All completed forms should sent to the Personnel Department.

THE FORM

The description of the form, and how to use it, will be specific to the organisation. The example discussed here refers to the form shown as Example 4 in Chapter 6.

Section 1 – Review of previous objectives

This section should be completed by the appraisee before the interview. The objectives cover those agreed at the last appraisal and should include any subsequent changes agreed at interim reviews. You should provide whatever help is necessary to the appraiser in completing this part of the form.

Section 2 – Performance rating

The appraisal form provides descriptions of the *lowest score indicator* and the *highest score indicator*. These indicators are provided as guidance for you in allocating a score for each rating. You should consider carefully the rating you give on each of the factors as the range of scores may differ greatly for each individual. It is entirely possible that an individual will score very low on some factors and very high on others. Even an average performer is unlikely to score 3 on every single factor. Appraisers should make every effort to use the full range of scores and not take an easy route by scoring 'down the middle'. It must be assumed that in every unit there will be a variation of scores awarded to different individuals. It is not possible to envisage, other than in very small units, that all the people will have performed to the same standard.

You should enter a score for each rating and work out the average score overall and enter this in the appropriate box.

The average score should then be converted into the overall performance rating; this overall score should represent what you consider to be the most appropriate rating for this individual. This score will not necessarily be the same as the arithmetic score but it would be surprising if there was not a clear relationship.

Section 3 – Overall performance rating

As the appraiser you have the authority to override the arithmetic score and should justify your decision in writing. In doing this you may wish to take other factors not considered in the previous section into account. It may include comments on aspects of personality or appearance or on an individual's attendance record. You may also want to take into account how well the appraisee performed on the achievement of the previous objectives, if appropriate.

In completing this section you should be as specific as possible and offer evidence for your judgements wherever you can. If, for example, an objective has been half achieved this should be stated.

Section 4 – Objectives for the coming year

Careful thought should be given to the selection of objectives for the coming year. You should not set more than four objectives for any individual. Objectives must be clearly stated and avoid vagueness. The use of words like *better* or *improvement* are not helpful as it is difficult to attach a measure to them. All objectives should be measurable, quantifiable and fair: for example, the achievement of higher revenue or lower cost; a faster turnaround or an increase in accuracy from *x* to *y*. Objectives can cover any element of the employee's job and should be relevant to the needs of the individual and the company. It may also be appropriate to set an objective which relates to the development of the individual.

The objectives agreed should be realistic and within the control of the employee. Failure to achieve objectives will not necessarily result in a poor appraisal score in the following year, but if correctly set they will give a strong indication of performance.

Section 5 – Potential and development

In this section you are asked to assess the potential of the individual to progress and to identify training needs which may help to develop skills and improve performance. It is important to make sure that the individual states their desire for career development and progress. You should start with a discussion about the appraisee's aspirations and training needs. Try to make sure that aspirations are realistic and meet your assessment of the progress you can envisage for this individual.

Move on then to a discussion about potential. Remember that not everyone will want to progress and this should not prevent them achieving a high rating on performance. You may need to reassure some individuals about this.

Complete the rating scale for potential.

CONCLUSION

You have a significant responsibility to ensure that the appraisal is a motivating experience for all employees and the more you encourage their involvement the more this will be the case.

Appendix B

EMPLOYEES' GUIDE TO APPRAISAL

WHY APPRAISAL?

Caught up in the day-to-day routine of the job it is sometimes difficult to take time to look at the job you are doing and assess how you can improve your performance, or find the opportunity to think about the long term and where you want your career to take you.

An appraisal provides a once-a-year opportunity to stand back and take stock. It is an opportunity for you to discuss with your manager how you are doing, talk about any problems you may be experiencing and make some plans for the future. The company benefits by hearing your views and providing guidance and training where it is most appropriate.

THE APPRAISAL SYSTEM

Our system has two main elements:

- **The appraisal form.** The form has been designed to cover the most important parts of your job and contains sections which will consider:

    - assessing your performance in the last period;

    - assessing your potential for development;

    - setting objectives for you to work for in the next period.

- **The appraisal interview.** The interview will be conducted by your appraiser who will be your manager or supervisor, who works closely with you an a daily basis. The interview will take place after you have both had time to consider the process and complete the appraisal form.

THE PROCESS OUTLINED

1.   *Completing your part of the appraisal form*

Your appraiser will give you the appraisal form in May and you will have a week to complete and return it.

You should start by reading the form and getting to understand it. An important part of the process is for you to complete a Self-Appraisal. You are asked to assess your performance over the last year and decide, on a rating scale, how well you have performed. You should also think about appropriate objectives for next year.

Self-appraisal is not compulsory – you have to choose to do it. However, the appraisal is yours and your full involvement means that it will be more likely to meet your needs.

Think carefully about your appraisal and complete the form in a quiet period at work or at home.

The interview will normally take place one week after you return the form to your appraiser and a suitable time will be arranged, giving you ample time to prepare. As part of your preparation you should note down any points you want to raise at the interview. The interview is intended to provide for a full and frank discussion of your performance and your feelings about your job and to discuss your ambitions and any problems you may be experiencing.

It will cover a number of key areas including:

- the key areas of your job comparing your ratings with those of your appraiser with a discussion of possible reasons for differences;

- your potential for future development and career progression;

- any training needs you may have;

- objectives to be set for the coming year.

Objectives

This section of the form asks you to assess how well you consider you have achieved the objectives which were set for you last year. This section will not be so relevant if you did not receive an appraisal last year and therefore have not been set any objectives. It will, however, be more important in future years.

Performance rating

The most important part of your self-appraisal is rating your past performance on the rating factors. You are asked to give yourself a rating between 1 and 6 for each factor depending on how well you believe you have performed. Each factor should be considered separately and because you believe that you should score high on one will not necessarily mean that you score high on all.

Read the description of the best and worst characteristics shown for each and think about how you performed.

Think seriously about your own performance and decide if you tend towards the higher end of the scale, a 4 or 5, the lower end, a 1 or 2, or are you in the middle? Make your decision and mark your score in the self-appraisal box. If you feel that any of the factors do not apply to your job, leave them and move on to the next, making a note of them for discussion at your interview.

It is hard to be completely objective about your own performance, but you should try to be as honest as possible in your assessment. You will have an opportunity to discuss your ratings with your appraiser at the interview. By that time, your appraiser will have given you a rating and you will compare the two. Don't just rate yourself randomly as you will need to be able to justify your scores.

Potential and development

This section is about your training, development and potential. You need to think what it is you want to achieve in the short and the longer term – where you want your career to take you. You will discuss this with your appraiser.

You are asked to rate your potential. Have you the potential to progress to a senior position in the organisation? If you do not believe you have the capacity or desire to progress, this will not be held against you in relation to your performance in your current job.

2. *Appraiser prepares ratings*

Once you have completed your parts of the form, you should return it to your appraiser who will go through it in the same way, assigning ratings for your performance on the scale. Your appraiser will also make an overall assessment of your performance, taking note of the arithmetical score but also taking into account other factors which are considered to be relevant to your performance throughout the year.

The appraiser will note his or her ratings in pencil as the scores may alter in the light of the discussion during the appraisal interview. At the same time the appraiser will prepare for the interview, noting your responses to the sections on objectives, rating and potential and development.

Setting objectives

Setting objectives for the coming period is an important element in the system and you and your appraiser should jointly agree up to four objectives which will help you to perform better in your job in the future. The purpose is to give you some measurable or specific targets to aim for during the coming year.

Instead of you and your appraiser simply agreeing, for instance, that you should *improve* in some way, you will jointly identify some clearly defined way of achieving an improvement.

Objectives should always be measurable – we should be able to identify clearly when they have been achieved.

When you have agreed your objectives for the year they will be noted on your appraisal form and you will be asked to sign to signify that you agree with them. These objectives will then be reviewed next year or earlier if appropriate and you will be asked to comment on how well you believe you performed in achieving them.

3. *Signing the appraisal form*

Once your appraiser has decided on your ratings he or she will ink in the scores and ask you to sign the form. Your agreement is required particularly in regard to the objectives for next year. If there are still some issues to be resolved at the end of the interview which your appraiser may want to discuss with his or her manager, or if your appraiser wishes to reconsider some ratings, you will be asked to sign the form at a later date.

If any disagreement cannot be resolved between you and your appraiser or your appraiser's manager, you will have the right to appeal, using the normal grievance procedure.

If you wish, your appraiser will give you a copy of your completed form.

4. *Your appraiser's manager countersigns the form*

Your appraiser's manager will review the form and the ratings and if they agree with the points made will countersign the form.

If there is any disagreement about ratings or other points on the form or the manager wishes to add any comments he or she will add them to the bottom of the form.

If changes are made to your overall performance rating you will be informed.

5. *Forms sent to Personnel Department*

The countersigned form will go on record as the Company's judgement on your performance during the past year and your potential for the future.

BIBLIOGRAPHY

Fletcher, C. (1993) *Appraisal: Routes to Improved Performance*, Institute of Personnel Management, London.

Fowler, A. (1990) Performance Management: the MBO of the 90s, *Personnel Management,* July.

Mumford, A. (1989) *Management Development: Strategies for Action*, Institute of Personnel Management, London.

Stewart, V. and Stewart, A. (1977) *Practical Performance Appraisal*, Gower.

Stewart, A. (1994) Performance Appraisal, *Handbook of Training and Development*, 2nd edn, edited by Prior, J., Gower.